T0329454

KENTUCKIANA ROADS

KENTUCKIANA ROADS

A FREIDENKER'S STORY OF LIFE IN AMERICA'S FLYOVER MIDDLE

RICK HOFSTETTER WITH JANE SIMON AMMESON

Algora Publishing
New York

Library of Congress Cataloging-in-Publication Data —

Names: Hofstetter, Richard R., 1956- author.
Title: Kentuckiana Roads: a Freidenker's story of life in America's flyover middle
  / Rick Hofstetter.
Other titles: Kentuckiana, a Freidenker's story of life in America's flyover
  land | Freidenker's story of life in America's flyover middle
Description: New York: Algora Publishing, [2017] | Includes index.
Identifiers: LCCN 2017001188 (print) | LCCN 2017003307 (ebook) | ISBN
  9781628942675 (soft cover: alk. paper) | ISBN 9781628942682 (hard cover:
  alk. paper) | ISBN 9781628942699 (pdf)
Subjects: LCSH: Brown County (Ind.)—Social conditions—21st century. |
  Indiana—Rural conditions—21st century. | Brown County (Ind.)—Social
  life and customs—21st century. | Brown County (Ind.)—Politics and
  government—21st century. | United States—Politics and government—21st
  century. | Rural population—Indiana—Attitudes. | Story Inn (Brown
  County, Ind.) | Hofstetter, Richard R., 1956- |
  Freethinkers—Indiana—Biography. | American wit and humor—Indiana.
Classification: LCC F532.B76 H6383 2017 (print) | LCC F532.B76 (ebook) | DDC
  977.2/253—dc23
LC record available at https://lccn.loc.gov/2017001188

Printed in the United States

To Ole and Joan Olson
and
To this proposition:
Nothing is sacred, but the power of reason.

ACKNOWLEDGMENTS

Writing any book is a personal journey, and that is especially true when the author writes it in the first person, as I have done here. But no book can be written without help from other people, which, true to my Catholic upbringing, now leaves me feeling a bit guilty, and immodest, for using the first person.

I cannot thank Jane Simon Ammeson enough for her counsel and guidance in writing this book, and, of course, for making many of the experiences that are recorded here possible in the first place. We decided a long time ago to write a book together, but as this book slowly took shape in my mind, it took a decidedly personal turn, which compelled me to adopt the first person and putatively become its sole author.

Jane, truly, this book would not have come into existence without you.

Thanks, too, to my buddy Frank Mueller. Frank and I embarked upon a journey to save a historic building, the Athenaeum, and then the historic town of Story. Both stand today as monuments to the success of those endeavors. Though technically Frank ceased to be a partner at the Story Inn eight years ago, he remains a valuable mentor and we remain the best of friends. *Immer Gemütlichkeit!*

Special thanks to my ersatz parents, Ole (the "Pontiff of Palate") and Joan Olson. Their wine tutorials proved to be invaluable in the early years of the Story Inn. They proved to be a steady hand when I needed it the most, launching first our monthly wine dinners and then the Indiana Wine Fair. Joan studied culinary arts in Paris with Julia Child, and she can make a much better meatloaf than my real mom. Ole and Joan are Freidenkers, too.

Thanks as well to Ruth Reichmann and Giles Hoyt. Ruth and Giles spent a good deal of their academic careers educating the public on the role of German immigrants in Indiana's history. We became acquaintances, then friends, 30 years ago when Ruth, Eberhard Reichmann (deceased) and Giles together formed the Indiana German Heritage Society. Ruth, Eberhard and Giles made it possible for me to appreciate Kentuckiana from an entirely new perspective. To use a hackneyed phrase: they helped me to "Identify German." That's good, because I had ditched another part of my identity, that of being Catholic.

Four organizations were generous in providing information and photographs to make this book possible: Historic Landmarks in Indianapolis, the Brown County Historical Society in Nashville, the TC Steele Museum in Brown County, and the Lilly Library at Indiana University in Bloomington. I am grateful for all these organizations do to keep Hoosier history alive.

Thanks, too, to Nelson Price. Nelson has written extensively about famous Hoosiers, interviewing many of them himself, and in the process, he has become an encyclopedia of all things Hoosier. Nelson hosts an hour-long radio show each week on WICR Indianapolis, called "Hoosier History Live." We've been friends since Ronald Reagan occupied the White House.

Thanks, finally, to the late James ("Doc") Counsilman. Were it not for Doc and his mentoring, I would likely have never set foot in Kentuckiana and may not have gone on to law school. Doc and his wife Marge were unabashed atheists, and would be pleased to see that I have finally come out of that closet and resisted becoming a Unitarian.

—Rick Hofstetter

1. Baptism at Pike's Peak. *Credit: Frank Hohenberger, thanks to the Brown County Historical Society*

TABLE OF CONTENTS

INTRODUCTION

I first met Rick Hofstetter on my second visit to Story. Several decades before, I had stumbled upon it on a drive with some friends from Bloomington, where we were all attending Indiana University. The town was tired, and the homes appeared ramshackle and abandoned. The general store, built in 1916, was still open, but barely so, a weather-beaten place with gas pumps topped with crowns that you no longer see at gas stations, and a hand pump out front with a cup tied to it for people to help themselves to a drink of water. Inside, I remember it being dark and dusty, the screen door slamming behind us as we walked into a large room with a wood burning stove installed the same year the store was built. I can't remember if we bought the pickled bologna that the then owner was famed for, but we did get a cold pop from the Coke machine, an antique even back then.

Years later, I read that the old General Store was now an inn and destination restaurant and that the homes comprising Story had become guest quarters. And so I made my way down the winding, twisting country roads that seemed to get narrower with each hairpin turn until I made the last curve in the road and saw Story again. But this time there was life to the town. A white horse and carriage stood in front and before I could make my way into the inn, the friendly carriage driver asked if I wanted to take a ride.

This section of Southern Indiana is breathtakingly beautiful with its dense copse of woods, hills and hollows (they really do call them "hollers" here), century-old homes and barns, pastures filled with grazing horses and meandering creeks. There's a sense of it being a small moment in time preserved in amber, a sense which one feels more intensely if you travel here as people did 150 years ago. I can understand why many people still travel to

Story by horseback. I have always loved Story and the land around it, and I always will.

Like the first trip to Story, my second trip was driven by curiosity. As a travel and food writer, I wanted to write about the village of Story and to learn how Rick and his former partner, Frank Mueller, had saved it from becoming a ghost town. During the course of my writing stories for magazines and newspapers, Rick and I discovered we shared a passion for historic and rural architecture, caves, quaint towns and the back roads of Indiana. I also, though Rick less so, love old cemeteries and the window they give on the lives of those buried there.

Over the years, we've traveled along these byways, learning more about Hoosier history and expanding into other states as well. It has been a journey of exploration and adventure, one which captures our passion for what has been.

And while we traveled, Rick's take on things which very much sums up his personality—witty, sardonic, curmudgeonly and super intelligent—was always the right travelogue that helped make what I call "Road Trips" with Rick even more exciting.

Working on this book with Rick is like being on the road with him again. It's been a trip I've loved to take.

Jane Simon Ammeson

PREFACE

On February 14, 1999, I bought a town.

Don't be impressed. It was a very small town in a very obscure place, located in the poorest township of the poorest county in one of this country's poorest states—Indiana. It didn't come with any people, either. The 13th Amendment to the United States Constitution made it illegal to buy a human being a long time ago.

Technically, it wasn't even a town, either. Story, Indiana was never incorporated as a municipality. But for some reason, it has appeared on maps since the mid-19th century. I'll never understand cartographers. There are a great many things that I do not understand. If I meet a cartographer someday, I intend to ask them why Canada is always pink.

I didn't even buy the town by myself. My good buddy Frank Mueller and I bought it together, at a sheriff's sale. There were no other bidders.

And I wasn't even there to do the bidding. I was in Strasbourg, France, courting the woman who would eventually become my third ex-wife. It was Frank who had our collective backs that day.

But together, Frank and I became the owners of a nearly 24-acre tract that was once a thriving logging and farming community, replete with a General Store building, an old wood-shop, grain mill, some barns, and several old homesteads dating back to the 19th century.

Story, Indiana, had fallen on hard times during the Great Depression, when virtually all of the population fled to Indianapolis and places beyond in search of jobs. The town was electrified in 1949, four years after the United States had acquired the technology to successfully irradiate two Japanese cities. Story's General Store limped along until the Nixon Administration, offering Nehi soft drinks, Moon Pies, and such local delicacies as pickled bologna served on snowy white Bunny Bread. Red and Gold Crown pumps dispensed leaded gasoline at pre-OPEC prices. A rusted hand-activated water pump stood outside with a tin cup attached. Everyone was allowed to take a drink, no charge for that. Sanitation seems not to have been a priority.

2. *Wheels of commerce rolling*

At its absolute nadir, in 1980, Story was purchased and repurposed by a hippie couple from nearby Bloomington, who had the vision to look at a derelict town and see a destination country inn. Their names were Benjamin and Cynthia Schultz, and by that I mean Benjamin, and Cynthia Schultz. Benjamin had no legal last name.

And that is how the Story Inn was born, a business whose name is identical to the town itself.

Benjamin and Cynthia made a good go of it, and conceived and gave birth to their children in the rooms above the General Store. (The General Store is now a restaurant and the rooms which proved to be so fecund are now guest accommodations.) But the hospitality business is consuming of both time and capital, so they sold the whole village to another couple in 1994. That couple lacked the vision of Benjamin and Cynthia, as well as their culinary or management expertise, and before long the Inn/town was in bankruptcy, receivership and, ultimately sold at sheriff's sale to the only suckers who would have it.

That would be Frank and me.

Fortunately, Frank had worked in the restaurant business, owning several, for four decades before retiring. I, rather cockily, assumed that my years of experience as a business lawyer would have some relevance to the challenge before us.

The early years were rough. The law of entropy was much in evidence in Story. Putting the train back on the tracks consumed more capital than I had lost through my first two divorces, and eventually, all of the capital I had to my name. Frank matched me dollar for dollar, in stoic German fashion.

I often surmise that one reason Frank and I get along so well is our common nationality—Frank was born in Germany during the waning days of the Third Reich; I was born in Pennsylvania, or rather assembled in Pennsylvania, mostly with German parts, and had a mother who at times could have gone toe to toe with Adolf Hitler and won.

Thus, neither one of us is "from" Indiana, but we each made Indiana our home by choice. Frank came here in 1968, to watch the "500" Race. He met a pretty girl, and as these things happen she became pregnant, and they married and hatched out three Hoosier girls who then, in turn, added grandchildren to the family tree. He also found time amidst all this breeding to open two successful restaurants and turn around the legendary Rathskeller in the Athenaeum building in downtown Indianapolis. He remains married to the same woman today, which might explain why his capital is still intact.

I came here in 1975, to attend Indiana University on a swimming scholarship, at the behest of the legendary coach James "Doc" Counsilman. Doc was the most successful college coach in any sport of all time, and cultivated the talents of Mark Spitz, Frank McKinney, Gary Hall, Jim Montgomery, Chet ("The Jet") Jastremski, and many, many others. Upon graduation, I made a few side trips, most notably to Durham, North Carolina, to attend Duke Law School. But eventually I returned to Indiana, and produced four Hoosier children by two different women. I supported these extravagances by practicing business law, which is only marginally more respectable than practicing the world's oldest profession, and less profitable.

As it turned out, my experience at Indiana University was invaluable. It was a gradual introduction to the place called Kentuckiana. College towns like Bloomington are characteristically full of hip and open-minded people, no matter where they might be. Or at least they were back in the 1970s, before stifling political correctness took hold on most campuses. Nobody back then gave much thought to gender-neutral bathrooms or "micro aggressions," as I recall. Back in the 1970s IU was a bit of an oasis, but on the occasions I left campus, I became aware of a very different world consisting of manufactured homes, Pentecostal churches, limestone quarries and gun stores.

Frank very sensibly wanted to pursue an exit plan, and in 2004 I obliged him by buying him out and quitting my law practice. Thus began my career as an innkeeper.

Compared to practicing law for a living, running an inn has been a joy. Gone are the suits and ties which brand lawyers as automatons. Gone is the hermetically-sealed office and the phalanx of legal assistants to screen people from meeting you. Small wonder that lawyers are arrogant, clueless, and universally loathed.

Today, I commute to work by foot, and it takes less than a minute. I don't own a watch or an alarm clock anymore.

Literally anyone can walk in the door of the Inn, and many interesting people do, even in this, the most benighted spot in Indiana.

Our guests have included US Vice President Mike Pence (in the spirit of full disclosure, he was merely Indiana's Governor the time he last visited); former Indiana Governor and current Purdue University President Mitch Daniels; Representative (now US Senator) Todd Young; at least three federal judges; at least three Indiana Supreme Court Justices; at least one Nobel Laureate; at least one billionaire; and, by our best estimate, six Rhodes Scholars and five university presidents (not including Mitch Daniels, lest he be counted twice). It's amazing how little attention such people command, compared to the stir we get when John Mellencamp, Bob Knight or one of the Indiana Pacers comes to visit. I've found that most accomplished people make interesting conversation.

I have not owned a television since Ronald Reagan was president, and spend way too much time reading stuff that would bore any normal person to tears. One evening in the Tavern, I struck up a conversation with an engaging and unassuming gentleman. We both liked Malbec. After about 30 minutes, I remarked to him that he "looked familiar." That's when I learned that I had been conversing with John Stehr, for two decades the news anchor at an Indiana network television affiliate.

So now, in my seventh decade of life, I have to admit that I might be at risk of becoming not just eccentric but reclusive as well. I get to meet some interesting people here, but I don't get out much.

That's why I must thank my companion Jane Simon Ammeson.

Jane is an accomplished travel writer and author, who attended Indiana University as well. A few years back, Jane wrote a series of flattering travel pieces on the Story Inn. Jane is a "progressive" in her political beliefs. I am steadfastly stuck in the 18th century's version of liberalism. Despite her political naïveté, Jane and I became fast friends.

Thanks to Jane, I did begin to get out occasionally, while she was "on assignment" in Kentuckiana. As a Progressive from greater Chicago, Jane finds Kentuckiana to be a strange and exotic place worth study, and I could not resist, with tongue firmly planted in cheek, comparing her to another Jane, named Goodall, for similar work she did in Tanzania. Without Jane, I would have gone to my grave without sleeping at the Iron Gate in Madison, or visiting the final resting spot of Jane Story (old cemeteries are a favorite of hers), or taking a tour of the Buffalo Trace Distillery or a subterranean boat ride in the Bluespring Caverns. It's a "bucket list" for me, and I was happy to be along for the ride.

Jane also urged me to write this book, perhaps for therapeutic reasons (she's also a psychologist).

If flyover America is a "Bible Belt," then Kentuckiana is its buckle. For years, I concealed my irreligiosity from parents, then friends and colleagues, the way transgender persons would hide their identity at a Harley Davidson rally. No more. Since I had no stomach to run for cover and become a Unitarian in nearby Bloomington, it was time to cut bait. This book is also my official "coming out" as a non-believer.

Isn't that what life's all about, going along for the ride, on our way to the end of the road, no matter where it may lead us?

PART I: JOURNEYS LOCAL

Chapter 1. The LGM

Take a mind-trip for a moment back into recent geologic time, to the late Pleistocene, a mere 22,000 years ago. Imagine, further, that you are seated in a Boeing 787 Dreamliner, at a window seat on the left side of that aircraft, and that this plane is en route from someplace on the east coast that's going to be important someday, to someplace on the west coast that's going to be important someday. As the first person to experience a "flyover" of what would become America's forgotten and benighted heartland, what would you see?

That plane would roughly be following the edge of a massive glacier. From your lofty perch, as you nibbled a diminutive bag of pretzels, you would be able to scan south, over hilly terrain unscarred by that glacier. The plane would almost certainly be buffeted by winds caused by the clash of warm and cold air, and so the pilot would turn on the "fasten seatbelt" sign so as not to bait the plaintiff's bar. To the north, if you could catch a glimpse out of a window on the right side of the plane while tethered to your seat, you would see a hellish frozen wasteland of solid ice, miles deep in places, that would extend all the way to the earth's north pole.

The earth has seen numerous glaciations over countless millennia, this being only the most recent. On that day, you would be witnessing the "Last Glacier Maximum," or LGM, of the "Wisconsin Glacial Episode."

At some point, the plane would pass over what would become Brown County, Indiana. At a cruising speed just shy of 600 miles per hour, it would take about four minutes for your plane to traverse the county from east to west.

If you could look straight down while you passed over, you would see a topography that wouldn't be a whole lot different from the one that exists today (despite being hemmed in to the north by a formidable wall of ice). However, it wouldn't look at all familiar. There wouldn't be a single church, manufactured home, convenience store, hunting stand, meth lab, shooting range, marijuana patch, tavern, Dixie flag or motorcycle rally to behold.

Humans migrated from Siberia to the Americas well before the LGM. But if there were people living in Brown County at the time while you passed by, there would no evidence of them at all. The first solid evidence of human habitation dates from about 13,000 years ago, and we only know them as the "Clovis People," for the apparent reason they gathered cloves. We know very little else about them.

Nevertheless, the Wisconsinan LGM left a lasting impression upon the people who would later populate Indiana. Today, the people of Brown County disdainfully refer to residents of the northern two thirds of the state as "flatlanders." I won't go into what folks in the north think of us, but it is rather snobbish, having much to do with cigarette consumption, bad teeth, and an aesthetic taste for derelict vehicles in front yards. A syndicated cartoonist named Kin Hubbard was largely responsible for creating that stereotype a half-century ago, and there's more than a corn-kernel of truth to it.

In Indiana, and throughout America's flyover heartland, there is a profound divide at the LGM. Whether the massive glacial footprint had anything to do with it or not is a matter of conjecture. Topographically, linguistically, ethnically, racially, genotypically, phenotypically, metaphorically, linguistically and, most redundantly, culturally, Indiana changes at that line. You can see it from a plane window. You can see it from space. But nowhere is it more evident than when you are on the ground.

The stereotypical image of Indiana—a tidy white farmhouse (replete with a barn, silo and windmill), situated on a broad flat plain that is lushly carpeted with Monsanto's GMO corn or soybeans—is accurate, to the extent stereotypes can ever be accurate, only north of the LGM. That's the image you see on the state's bicentennial stamp. The receding glacier simultaneously acted like a great steamroller and conveyor belt, both flattening the landscape as it thrust forward, and fertilizing it with jetsam from Michigan and Canada as it receded.

In Lafayette, well to the north of the LGM, the soil is as black as a fresh cow patty, and just as fertile. Plant a seed and jump back. The Indiana south of the LGM is very different. It is hilly, and the brown soil so bereft of nourishment that it can barely sustain a cannabis patch without constant, loving care.

In this manner, the glacier severed the southern one third of Indiana from the rest of the state.

It is a myth that Indiana is anything more than a political concoction, and I say that with great remorse, as this state celebrates its bicentennial. Indiana joined the union at the same time as Missouri, in a compromise that would balance one free state for each slave state added to the growing country. I'm proud to say that Indiana was one of the former.

But the state is roughly twice as tall as it is wide (if you assume, as cartographers do, that north is "up"), and a lot happens as you travel from north to south. Comparing Evansville in the extreme south to Gary in the north would be disingenuous. Indianapolis sits smack in the center of the state, about 50 miles north of the LGM. It is a flattened landscape that is stereotypically Indiana. With few topographical obstacles to overcome, the city was laid out with streets at right angles, true to the points of the compass, all in keeping with the orderly but aesthetically-challenged minds of the mostly German people who settled there. Economically and culturally, it dominates the region, a place unto itself.

Thus, it's taken two centuries and no one has yet to define what a "Hoosier" is. The term is broad enough to include wandering Germans like Frank and me as well as families with roots as deep as an old growth oak. It is broad enough to include anyone who watches Indiana basketball, wherever they might be. (Like Pittsburgh, Indiana is an exporter of people, and the diaspora may be recognized by their team loyalties.) "Hoosier" makes for a suitable name for an athletic team in this era of stifling political correctness, because no one knows what a "Hoosier" is, and thus, there are no thin-skinned people out there to feel offended when one affixes it to an athletic team. The same is true for "Steelers."

Everything changes at the LGM. To the north of the LGM is "Urbania," a territory of mostly flat farmland dominated by Indianapolis, where everyone wears blue jerseys bearing a distinctive representation of a horse shoe, and drives their cars in circles. To the north and west of Urbania is "Iliana," dominated by Chicago, a real city where cops kill, on average, 50 citizens a year. Due north of Urbania is "Michiana," a territory distinguished by the largest bodies of fresh liquid water on the planet (a gift of the receding glacier). Michiana used to be dominated by a great city, Detroit, but the people there got lead poisoning and moved away. To the east of Urbania is "Ohiana," which has no distinguishing features other than an interstate highway that mercifully allows one to traverse it quickly.

To the south of the LGM lies "Kentuckiana," a territory that extends beyond the Ohio River well into bourbon country, and embraces Louisville and, by most accounts, the fringes of Cincinnati. It is a hill country full of moonshiners, Harley riders, horsemen, hardscrabble farmers and a noticeable dearth of dentists. If Kentuckiana were to be a separate state, it would still be legal to smoke inside schools and hospitals. Further south, Kentuckiana fades imperceptibly into Appalachiana, a forbidding place where people listen to banjo music and sheep run scared.

3. *A new perspective of Flyover America.*

The southern half of Indiana is roughly bisected, north to south, by State Road 135. In Indianapolis it is more appropriately known as Meridian Street. The Soldier's and Sailor's Monument in the center of downtown is as good a place as any to embark on a road trip from Urbania to Kentuckiana. The Monument was built to commemorate those who sacrificed their lives so our nation would not be torn asunder, and it is topped with a statue that appropriately faces south.

Suburban Indianapolis is as ugly, and featureless, as the suburbs are in any American city. But at some point, the strip malls and fast food joints give way to farms and small towns, and SR 135 morphs into a straight two-lane road with a true bearing south. Except for the occasional traffic light and school crossing, one can drive nearly as fast on SR 135 as on the interstate. That all changes at the LGM.

Kentuckiana begins, and Urbania ends, at a little village called Morgantown. SR 135 becomes the town's main street, and the cops stand ready to pounce. Morgantown is the first place on your journey south where you will see a Rebel flag displayed without any sense of irony. It flies in front of a biker dive bar called Frenchy's Pub on Main Street. Directly across the street from Frenchy's is Kathy's Café, a quintessentially Kentuckiana eatery. At Kathy's, you can enjoy meatloaf with whipped potatoes, and it will come with a piece of white bread crowned with a pat of genuine margarine. The pies are fresh and delicious. Kentuckianans know pie.

Morgantown has the requisite accouterments of any respectable Kentuckiana small town: a 19th century Christian church, a convenience store, post office, mortuary, liquor store, and a small grocery store. It *feels* like Kentuckiana. This is exactly where the glacier stopped. To the north, SR 135 is straight and true. To the south, you enter hill country, where the road twists and farms give way to forests. There's a century-old iron bridge at Morgantown. Cross that bridge, and you're in Kentuckiana. Just beyond that bridge is the northern border of Brown County.

SR 135 meanders south, all the way to the Ohio River. It connects a host of small towns, including Nashville, Story, Brownstown, and, finally, Corydon, Indiana's first state capital. South of Nashville, SR 135 becomes curvier, and far less trafficked. Sometimes, the road will take abrupt 90 deg. turns, the result of having yielded the right-of-way to farmers' fields. It is one of America's most scenic by-ways.

I would submit to you that there are practical reasons for re-drawing state lines to encompass topographical features or the cultural commonalities of the people who live there. But it is an exercise that is, for better or for worse, both impracticable and illegal. Article IV, Section 3, of the US Constitution provides: "no new State shall be erected or formed within the Jurisdiction of any other State; nor any State be formed by the Junction of two or more States, or Parts of States . . ." This would clearly prohibit the calving off of southern Indiana and the stitching of it onto northern and western Kentucky.

4. Time for a road trip.

For reasons which elude me, constitutional law scholars remained sanguine when West Virginia was hacked out of Virginia at the time of the Civil War. Perhaps there were other matters of a more pressing urgency. Or maybe the people of the genteel South just didn't want to be associated with Hillbillies.

There are a lot of things I do not understand. For example, I do not understand what people mean when they use terms like "living wage," "fair trade," "empowerment" and "sustainable." Or why banks even bother to have business lending departments these days. Or what it means to have a "free speech area" or a "safe place" on a university campus.

So, for the time being, southern Indiana will have to remain tethered to the rest of Indiana.

CHAPTER 2. THE STORY

> "When you arrive at a fork in the road, take it."
>
> —Yogi Berra

Story, Indiana, sits at the northern fringe of Kentuckiana, just a tobacco-spit from where the Wisconsinan glacier ran out of gas 22,000 years ago.

Kentuckiana was mostly populated with white people who arrived by that great inland water route, the Ohio River. It was a diverse lot from Europe, but dominated by two ethnic groups, the Germans and the Scotch-Irish. They began arriving in mass in the late 18th century and did not stop until the First World War, when it became unfashionable to be a German.

The Germans quickly established the cities and towns that dot each side of the Ohio River—Cincinnati, Madison, Louisville, Owensboro, Evansville, and many other communities, some of which struggle for survival today. These towns all had one thing in common: a brewery. Some, like Cincinnati, had multiple breweries.

The Scotch-Irish, meanwhile, pioneered inland from the Ohio, establishing working stills in every holler and a clapboard church at every crossroad.

Indiana was, of course, already populated with people when the Europeans arrived, and the relations between the natives and the newcomers predictably grew restless. This attitude persists today. Even though the ethnic makeup of the population has shifted decidedly since the 18th century, the natives of Kentuckiana are still suspicious of outsiders. When I arrived here in 1999, the locals thought I was from Mars. I, of course, thought them to be from a galaxy far, far away.

5. *"So how do we keep the leprechauns away"?*

Fortunately for the arriving Europeans, small pox and alcoholism had already thinned the herd. It took only a few masterful strokes of a pen to isolate, exterminate and/or relocate the indigenous population ahead of the demographic steamroller heading up from the south.

One such stroke-of-pen occurred in 1809, when then Governor of the Indiana territory William Henry Harrison signed a treaty with the Miami Indians, opening up three million acres of wilderness to European settlement

(Indiana didn't become a state until 1816, but when the title "Governor" was bestowed upon him, it didn't take a visionary to see where this was heading).

The so-called "Ten-O'clock Treaty" got its name because the boundary drawn to forever separate the Indian from the European territories was denoted by a shadow cast at a defined point at 10am on September 30. The line, running diagonally across Indiana from the mouth of Raccoon Creek of the Wabash River near Montezuma, to a place near Seymour, is still used today in the state's land survey descriptions. That's all that remains of the Ten O'Clock Treaty.

The Ten-O'Clock Line forms the southwest boundary of the Brown County State Park and runs right through the town of Story. It forms the boundary between the town and the park. Some years back, Benjamin and Cynthia Schultz brought a 23,000 lb. pillar of limestone to Story to mark the treaty line. Sculptor William Galloway fashioned the limestone into a tree with saws and tools, and a rifle, to depict the town's pioneer history.

We finished the project in 2000 by pouring a giant concrete sundial around that monument. The shadow cast at 10am on September 30 (you'll have to trust me on this) runs through an old wood shop at Story, which we dutifully renamed the "Treaty House." The Treaty House is one of our premier overnight accommodations, with an outdoor hot tub.

A few years ago, surveyors from the Indiana Department of Natural Resources set the line back about 15 feet, bequeathing to us an additional third of an acre. We're grateful for that gesture. Perhaps it was in appreciation for my services as an unpaid collector of state sales tax since 1999.

Story is located in southern Brown County, an inaccessible place even by Kentuckiana standards. The town currently has a permanent population of only three people and three dogs. But on a busy Saturday evening, as many as 40 additional people can be found occupying guest cottages. Some of those people bring dogs, too.

The most recent census puts about 15,200 people in Brown County, all but six of whom are white. It is the least populated, and easily the whitest, of Indiana's 92 counties. It is far whiter than any country in Europe, which is where white people came from. Brown County is also among the poorest of Indiana's counties, and Van Buren Township, where Story is situated, is easily the poorest township in Brown County. Impressive credentials.

Per capita, there are more people holding PhDs and gun permits than any other Indiana county. I would submit to you that there is almost no overlap between these two groups. Some portion of the former are affiliated with Indiana University, located due west. The rest of the PhDs, it seems, are either retired or, like my third ex-wife, will endure a long commute to Butler University in Indianapolis for the privilege of owning a horse.

There are 41 Christian churches in Brown County, no mosques or synagogues, and only three traffic lights. Story used to have a Christian church, too, but it's gone, along with the rendering plant and gas station.

There is only one incorporated town in all of Brown County: Nashville. It is a tourist village of 800 souls located a 13 serpentine mile drive to the north of Story. It is also the seat of county government, where the real power brokers reside. All three of the county's traffic lights are located a short distance from each other in Nashville. With some degree of planning, it is possible to avoid the power brokers, and the traffic lights, completely.

As Story is concerned, the newest building still standing predates electrification, and so it retains the feel of an authentic 19th century Midwestern small town. The Old General Store, a classic Dodge-City style frame building, still dominates the village. It's been repurposed into a restaurant, tavern and guest rooms. The other buildings in town which haven't burned down or succumbed to the law of entropy are now converted into guest cottages or facilities for weddings. These include an old wood shop (the one we renamed the "Treaty House"), an old grain mill, an old dairy barn, and several former private residences.

The prevailing architectural style at Story is "Vernacular," which is a kind of poor man's Victorian. Back in the 19th century, there wasn't much money for frills like gingerbread, bargeboard and fish-scale siding, so the houses are comparatively plain and simple. Every single building at Story, barns included, is a stick-built structure with a metal (previously shake) roof.

6. *Call a landscaper.*

The dearth of capital proved to be both a curse and a blessing for Story. With little money available to maintain its buildings, the place became drab and empty as the years took their toll. The General Store's metal exterior yielded to the elements and began to bleed rust, nearly obscuring the signage reading "Alra Wheeler General Merchandise, Story Ind." But mercifully there was no money to "modernize" its interior when people were doing awful things to old buildings back in the 1950s, '60s and '70s. No one attempted to cover the old tin metal ceiling with dropped fiberboard panels sporting fancy new recessed neon lightbulbs. No one attempted to affix asbestos floor tiles to its hardwood floors. No one tried to freshen up the old merchandise shelves or rolling ladder with a coat of lead-based paint. As a result, the General Store, and most of Story's structures, survived the decades with little more than scars and grime to show for it.

As a person who's spent a lot of time and money undoing other people's misguided efforts to modernize—things like covering clapboard with aluminum or vinyl siding—I cannot understand the premise that underlies the desire to tamper with fine old buildings in the first place. I also do not understand why the US Treasury still mints dollar coins and two dollar bills. Or why people salt their food before tasting it, or why someone would order a beef filet well-done.

Story hosts about 70 weddings per year, an impressive number since we lost our church some time ago. Today, destination weddings are all the vogue. Very sensibly, the United States Supreme Court has recognized marriage to be a fundamental right of couples, regardless of gender, and we cater to couples of all leanings. I personally officiated a wedding between two female employees, Dani Ham and Brittani Williams, in our lovely garden. Still, with three failed marriages of my own, it sometimes remains a mystery to me why people still want to get married at all, especially if the choice is between that and single life with an adoring dog.

A lot of babies are conceived at Story as well. As already noted, Benjamin and Cynthia Schultz conceived and birthed their children right there. Some years back, we solicited our guests to share with us their "conceivable stories" and were astounded with the response. One couple even named their little girl "Story."

There's no fertility clinic at Story. However, we do have a nice wine list and great Indiana artisan beers.

Story stands company with a number of other over-the-hill Brown County towns, some of them with strange names like Gnaw Bone, Bean Blossom, Stone Head, Helmsburg, Gatesville and Pike's Peak, all of which have withered to such an extent that Story looks bustling by comparison. However, at least a few have retained their churches.

Helmsburg, which lies about seven miles to the northwest of Nashville, actually has a sawmill as well as a church. Excluding portable sawmills, it's one of only two in Brown County still in operation. At one time sawmills dotted almost every stream and waterway in the county. Most of these have decayed and disappeared. Story's sawmill was lost, along with its school.

7. Gone, but not forgotten.

The Helmsburg sawmill is owned by a curmudgeon named Bill Pool, who may have started working there about the time the glacier receded at the end of the Pleistocene. I like him—maybe because I'm a fellow curmudgeon. Bill sells mostly rough-sawn poplar, harvested locally, which can be made into siding, fencing or tabletops. His prices are reasonable, too, as cheap or cheaper than you'll find at Menards, enabling you to save big money. As for his sartorial style, I'm guessing Bill has never worn anything but bib overalls, even to church.

Bean Blossom sits four miles due north of Nashville, a mere three miles east of Helmsburg, on a well-trafficked section of SR 135 carrying Flatlanders south desperately looking to buy caramel corn. Bean Blossom has a magnificent covered bridge in cherry condition, constructed in 1880. But you can't see it from the road. It sits a quarter mile to the west, and amazingly, it is still in service.

8. *Where's Opie?*

Kentuckiana has many surviving covered bridges. Brown County has another gem, circa 1838, about five miles from Bean Blossom, at the north entrance of the Brown County State Park.

In Bean Blossom, at the southwest corner of the intersection of SR 135 and SR 46 (no traffic light) sits a must-see attraction, an overstocked antique store known as Plum Creek Antiques, owned by a delightful couple, Paul and Paulette. Very close to that, to the south, is the highly respected Bean Blossom Animal Clinic, run by Dr. Brester, a modern-day Dr. Dolittle. Dr. Brester is the most overworked veterinarian in the world. Brown County pet owners swamp his clinic from morning to evening, because he is good, kind, and bizarrely inexpensive. Some years back, he put down Jane's dog Chocolate, gratis, after he had been run over by a Hillbilly on Blue Creek Road. Dr. Brester should be canonized a saint.

A quarter mile north of Paul and Paulette's place sits the Bill Monroe Music Park and Campground, the sight of unmitigated debauchery each September when it hosts the Bean Blossom Biker Fest. Bill Monroe also hosts marginally more respectable events featuring Bluegrass and Gospel music. Directly across the road from the Bill Monroe Music Park gate is a trailer park of dilapidated manufactured homes, and barely a quarter mile to the south of that incongruously sits an ancient white clapboard Mennonite Church, on which is painted: "Strangers Expected." Mennonites have a gift for understatement.

Two miles east of Bean Blossom is a quaint restaurant known as the "Farmhouse" located in a brick building built in the 1830s, with excellent food and a wonderful garden/greenhouse to stroll through. It's worth the trip, if you can find it—people often get lost as Brown County outlawed billboards and directional signs a long time ago, and the Farmhouse is well off the beaten trail.

East of the Farmhouse Restaurant, and equally inaccessible, is Gatesville, which has a quaint old general store plucked from the 1940s. The pies and cakes are fresh, home-made and delicious. There's not much else of notoriety at Gatesville, except the fact that it is the birthplace of my best friend, Snow, the product of an unarranged union between a German Shepherd and a Husky-like farm dog.

Nobody knows how Gnaw Bone got its name, but some folks speculate that it is a bastardization of "Narbonne" in France. The town is easy to mistake for a common-looking commercial stretch of Kentuckiana road, in a heavily trafficked section of SR 46 connecting Nashville to Columbus (Indiana) to the east. There's a gas station in Gnaw Bone, offering pork tenderloins (which are so famous that the "Today" show stopped by to film there), lottery tickets and, of course, cigarettes.

9. *"Slow down! Coming up on the town."*

Everyone born in Brown County smokes cigarettes. It's the law. Everyone in Brown County hunts, too. It's not the law to hunt, but the right to hunt is actually enshrined in Indiana's Constitution. I kid you not.

Gnaw Bone is home to the Brown County Winery, which makes an excellent port and a blush wine from Catawba that we sometimes sell at Story as a substitute for White Zinfandel (even we have scruples). You can sample these, and many others, in a handsome tasting room at the winery while you listen to the sound of steel-belted radials hitting pavement. Bear Wallow Distillery finds its home there, too, and you can sample spirits in a lovely tasting room bedecked with poplar cut by Bill Pool himself.

Gnaw Bone also has a gun store, which sells hunting and fishing accouterments too, connected to a shop which does small engine repair. This place bears no resemblance to the he-man outdoorsmen megastores you find at suburban shopping malls these days. There are no designer sportsmen clothes, but you can buy live night crawlers and crickets there, along with two-cycle oil for your lawnmower or weed-eater. Gnaw Bone has a Harley Davidson shop, a flea market, a campground (replete with an artificial fishing lake) and a farm feed store, making the place pretty much self-sufficient.

At this point I would pause and note some of Brown County's linguistic and cultural oddities, no doubt the product of the area's isolation and flyover status. In Standard American English, the verb "to eat" is irregular. ("I eat, I ate, I have eaten".) In Brown County, locals have made it into a regular verb, but only as it pertains to using a lawn tool known as a "weed eater." To communicate the fact that you have completed the task of trimming a ditch or gully of unwanted grass or weeds, you would say, "I weed-eated it."

People here also routinely add syllables to words. For example, "measured" as "may-jour-ed." The name "Jill" is pronounced "Gee-ill," "Bill" is "Bee-ill," "door" is "doe-oar," "beans" is "be-ans," "inch" is "eee-yinch" "beer" is "bee-ear," "mold" is "mode" (not quite two syllables, but heading that way) and "store" is "sto-oar."

Locals also employ the pronoun "me" in the first person, but only when they are attempting to invoke the plural. For example: "I'm goin' to the sto-oar" (singular) as opposed to "Gee-ill and me are goin' to the sto-oar" (plural).

If you live south of State Road 46 in Brown County, in Stone Head, Story or Pike's Peak, you'll discover a linguistic "vernacular" of its own. It's charming, if provincial, to hear a local resident refer to Nashville as "town." "I'm goin' to town" really means, "I'm going to Nashville." To the north, beyond the "town," is the "city," and the heart of Urbania. "I'm goin' to the city" means, "I'm going to Indianapolis." This study in geography is all that many people in this county know of what lies north of the LGM.

Blame it on bad schools. Or home-schooling. A young Noam Chomsky would have had a field day here (he's become a curmudgeon, and nearly irrelevant, in his old age as well).

South of SR 46, in Van Buren Township, you'll also encounter an odd custom. If you are driving a pick-up truck, EVERYONE who passes by will wave to you. It is customary, even rude, not to wave back in the same manner. And the wave is really more of a salute, with arm extended, with fingers configured in the shape of a pistol but "aiming" in a 45 degree angle upwards.

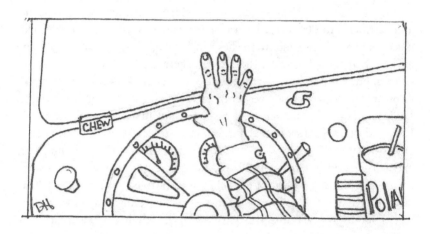

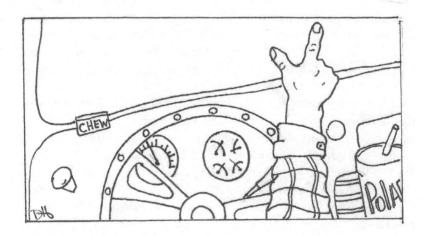

10. The "Van Buren wave."

If road conditions do not permit you to safely take your hands off of the wheel, four fingers on the right hand upraised will suffice. No one knows the origin of the "Van Buren Salute," but I suspect that it came into use because the chances are compellingly high that anyone driving a pick-up truck down there is either a neighbor or kin.

Stone Head sits seven miles south of Nashville, and five miles east of Story. It is named for a stone head, a not-so-flattering likeness of a guy who ran the Brown County Highway Department about 150 years ago. Back then, in lieu of paying highway taxes, you could work on the county road crew. The sculptor wanted to do neither, and bought himself a pass by carving a stone head. Again, I can't make this stuff up.

11. "I think I just saw it move."

Back in the 1970s someone stole the stone head, but it eventually resurfaced, to again be displayed in front of the "House at Stone Head," a very fine 1895 Victorian farmhouse where the road forks. Unfortunately, some local thugs took a sledge hammer to it on November 5, 2016, and made off with the bulk of it. If we are so fortunate to see it again, it will be in damaged condition.

Every now and then, a local meth-head makes off with our red and gold Standard Crowns from the retired gas pumps in front of the General Store. That makes a little bit of sense, because they're worth something to a crooked antique dealer somewhere, who will satisfy, however temporarily, the thief's drug cravings. But the broken head from Stone Head has no such value, making this act senseless.

Mike Kelly, a retired orthodontist and dedicated naturalist, and his wife Jan bought and restored the House at Stone Head a few years ago and built a delightful nature walk behind it. Slowly, they have rid the area of invasive species, restoring it into a pristine wetland consisting of many acres. Snow and I walk the verdant footpaths together regularly. Periodically, the creek (pronounced "cree-ick") at Stone Head floods, wreaking havoc. It is, after all, a wetland.

There's little else at Stone Head. The old service station is long gone, but Benjamin and Cynthia Schultz salvaged the old "Standard" sign, which has come to rest on the General Store building at Story. I paid a nominal price for the sign and issued a check made simply to "Benjamin."

At the end of the road west of Story is (or rather was) the town of Elkinsville. It disappeared entirely from the map in 1960, when the United States Army Corps of Engineers flooded the bottomland between Brown County and Monroe County to the west to create Lake Monroe. The lake severed Elkinsville Road, which once connected Story to Belmont via Elkinsville.

Today, little remains at Elkinsville but an old post office that has stood vacant for over five decades. A large cemetery, with more bodies in it than Elkinsville had living souls at its zenith, still sits atop a hill. Belmont, to the west, is little more than a boat ramp.

Elkinsville Road still bisects Story, but it dead-ends five miles to the west at a fallen iron bridge and a labyrinthine tangle of slow-moving tributaries, all called "Salt Creek." One can take a nice canoe ride on 50 miles of tributary when Salt Creek is flowing (skip July). By any measure, Salt Creek has the best fishing (locals say "fee-ish-ing") in Kentuckiana. Whatever your pleasure, bring mosquito repellant.

Some years back, a female goat escaped from a local farm and took up residence under a bridge at Salt Creek, less than a mile from Story. I'm not making this up. Miraculously, she survived hunting season, assisted by locals who found a convenient way to recycle their kitchen trash. Goats are not picky eaters. As winter set in, the goat moved into a nearby barn occupied by Puck, my soon to be third wife's quarter horse. Puck and the goat, now known as "Phoebe," then developed a peculiar bond and became inseparable.

Goats are destructive creatures and can make short work of the rag top on a late model BMW convertible, so eventually we thought it prudent to relocate Phoebe to a nearby farm, and local farmer Dean Manual was happy to oblige. Puck never forgave us, but Phoebe immediately found companionship with a male goat, and the couple produced a bunch of kids. Dean kept secret Phoebe's previous liaison with Puck.

Committed hikers may wish to climb "Browning Mountain," one of the highest points in Kentuckiana. The trailhead begins at the end of Elkinsville Road. At its top is a series of large stones, obviously hauled up there with great effort during pre-Columbian times. Theories abound as to who put them there, and why, but the prevailing theory is that it had some religious significance. The trail is entirely on public land, but local residents do not take kindly to people invading "their" space. Sometimes, even parking on Elkinsville Road, a public right-of-way, will incite the territorial instincts of the locals. I urge caution.

There's an old guy named Bill Miller who lives in a little cottage back there. He earned his credentials as a Progressive, decades ago, as a volunteer with the Peace Corps, and he now fancies himself to be the protector of the local ecosystem and a whole lot of other things. Progressives are always eager to assume the role of protectors. If Bill gives you a friendly pass to go up Browning Mountain, he may no longer remember you upon your return three hours later.

12. You are cleansed.

As a result of the Lake Monroe project, Bloomington, Indiana's sixth most populous city and the home of Indiana University, got a reliable water supply. Today, a limestone monument commemorates the destruction of this town by the power of eminent domain. Some folks believe that the flooding of Elkinsville was the inspiration behind the movie "Deliverance." Indeed, there are some scary people still living back there, and none of them looks much like Burt Reynolds or John Voight. (None of their daughters look much like Angelina Jolie, either.)

13. *"The art of medicine consists in amusing the patient while nature cures the disease."* — *Voltaire*

Though Brown County is thinly-populated, it has a lot of churches. A great number of them are small, simple white clapboard structures which date back to the 1800s. If Christianity is declining across the globe, there is no evidence of it in Brown County.

The people in Brown County are a fractious lot, but unlike many other places in the world, people here do not blow up planes or hack each other to pieces for religious reasons. It is inconceivable that the Pastor of the Christianburg Church, circa 1866, would issue a fatwa against the congregation choosing to attend the nearly identical-looking Pike's Peak Church of Christ, circa 1891, three miles away. Members of each congregation meet amiably for the annual fish fry at the Van Buren Township Fire Department, or at the County Fair. Some people date, and even marry, across congregational lines. Such mixed marriages are a cause for neither derision nor scorn in Brown County. When a Brown County girl becomes pregnant by someone outside of her tribe, there are no honor killings.

Some Brown County churches don't even exist as churches *per se*. There's a congregation that meets in the horseman's camp of the Brown County State Park each Sunday for worship services. Dean Manual, the same local farmer who gave refuge to Phoebe, hauls in the congregation's church-kit by means of a mule-drawn carriage. They call themselves "missionaries," even though everyone here has already been Christianized.

The pastors of the local churches will confer their blessing upon many inanimate objects, presumably to make them safe in this world—or the next. Before many large excursions, Harley Davidson riders will collect in mass to participate in a solemn ceremony known as "the blessing of the bikes." Go with the grace of God, *sans* helmet. A preacher's blessing will keep you safe from snakebite as well.

There are lots of graveyards in Brown County, too. Some of these are physically attached to the churches, but, curiously, most are orphaned. I have visited dozens of them with Jane, who has a morbid curiosity of such things. Jane will insist that I ditch the car some place where it could easily be wiped out by a piece of farm equipment and climb a steep hill to an unkempt, windswept place of haphazardly tilting tombstones which pre-date the Civil War. Sometimes, these trips are full of surprises.

It was when visiting the old cemetery on Christianburg Road that Jane and I discovered the gravestone of Jane Story, wife of Dr. George P. Story, who founded the town that still bears his name. Jane Story died on November 30, 1872, and she is laid to rest next to her baby who survived but one day. In the restaurant we proudly display the original land patent to Dr. Story, dated 1851, signed by President Millard Fillmore. It describes a 73.74 acre tract of land that straddled the Ten O'Clock Line.

14. The typical outcome of country medicine circa 1800s

15. A real Story is buried here.

One of these local cemeteries is the final resting spot of Alra Wheeler, the postmaster who rebuilt the general store in 1916 after an explosion destroyed it. For nine decades, local lore decreed that Wheeler had been shot while he was standing next to the pot belly stove in Story's General Store building. In fact, he died of cancer in a hospital in the early 1920s. Not much room for salacious gossip there.

Visiting graveyards gives a glimpse of life as it existed before the Internet, automobiles, the Jerry Springer Show, Duck Dynasty, or electricity. There are a prodigious number of children buried in Brown County, many without names, just sadly bearing the designation "infant" with a date of birth and death only a few days apart. Jane Story's baby is but one of them.

Birth rates were high back then, and so was infant mortality. Without question, there are more people below the dirt in Brown County than above it.

These headstones in old graveyards, every one askew and weathered, bear familiar names: Wilkerson, Hedrick, Greathouse, Tabor, Hamblin, Wheeler, Harden, Carmichael, Fleetwood, Ayres, Lucas—many still prominent among the living here in Brown County. Indeed, Francis "Pete" Wilkerson, whose family grew up here, has come out of retirement to work at the Story Inn. He is energized by his wife Jackie, our gardener. Both are cancer survivors and determined to make the most of every passing day. The fruit of their labors and considerable talents are much in evidence.

The family Lucas, by the way, is the same one that spawned Forrest Lucas, who founded Lucas Oil Products, one if Indiana's most successful companies. (Lucas purchased naming rights to the stadium where the Indianapolis Colts play with deflated balls.) I would be remiss in not mentioning that my own son-in-law hails from the Lucas clan. But overall, there's been an undeniable out-migration of talented people from Brown County, which has done little to enrich the local gene pool.

16. *Forrest Lucas, a good one who got away.*

Judging from the grave markers, those surviving the first five years of life stood a pretty good chance of living to a ripe old age. Being of a ripe old age myself, sometimes I wonder if it's worth the effort to go home after visiting one of these local cemeteries. (This assumes that I could remember how to get back home from there, or recall what I was doing in a graveyard in the first place.) Perhaps I'll have my remains interred in one of them someday, after the EPA finds a safe place to dispose of my liver.

Sadly, the old graveyards of Brown County are in a deplorable state. They're supposed to be maintained by the Township Trustees but are sorely neglected because dead people don't complain much. Some years back, one such Trustee from Van Buren Township absconded with taxpayer money and spent it all on a personal holiday at Dollywood, in Pidgeon Forge. Dollywood sits in a dry county, well within Appalachiana.

Talk about senseless crimes. The presence of so many dead people, and a few live ones with fertile imaginations, has led to a multitude of ghost sightings. Story is perhaps best known for its resident ghost, the "Blue Lady."

Each of the hotel rooms at Story is appointed with a guest book, where people may record their poetry, and profundities, gossip and foibles. When

Frank and I bought Story, I poured over guest books dating back to the early 1980s and found, to my astonishment, that the guest books from a certain room, then called the "Garden Room," contained consistent reports of ghost sightings.

When a guest book is finally filled up with blather, they are typically put into storage and replaced with a clean guest book, so that the process can resume. I found the SAME REPORTS in DIFFERENT GUEST BOOKS, spanning two decades. These recordings were made by different people at different times, under circumstances when they could not possibly have communicated with each other. (I find it difficult to believe that guests were skulking through the attic at night, pouring over archived books). Somehow, the name "Blue Lady" stuck.

I am a skeptic and fancy myself to be an empiricist as well. I cannot explain how these reports came into existence, but then again, there are a whole lot of things about life that I do not understand. Things like "negative" interest rates, or why Germany gave up the mark. Or what it means when they put a cop on "administrative leave."

Now the fact that we have observations that cannot be immediately explained is not proof of a ghost. We need a hypothesis, and then we must test that hypothesis. If the hypothesis is untestable, then it's time look for a new hypothesis. I will believe in the Blue Lady if, and when, we successfully summon her for a deposition and a blood draw. Until then, I will continue to refuse to believe my own eyes. It could be the spirits in the basement (86 proof, or even higher) that could be accounting for these observations. That hypothesis, at least, is a testable one.

Of course, being the shameless promoter that I am, I posted some of these guest book entries on the newly-minted Internet, and renamed that room the "Blue Lady Room." Sad to say, this was all the empirical evidence that many people needed to be convinced of her existence. The power of reason cannot stamp out this meme, any more than it can stop sick people from visiting Lourdes for a cure. However, I will cynically say that the pilgrimages to Story have proved to be profitable.

The legend of the Blue Lady has brought pilgrimages of a different sort. Slews of ghost tracking societies have conducted "investigations" here with equipment that looks decidedly high-tech. Almost all of those studies "confirm" the presence of visual or auditory "anomalies." Their pseudo-scientific "findings" can be found all over the Internet. They give credence to the people who require little of evidence to reach the conclusion that a ghost is behind it all.

Me, I remain as unpersuaded as ever. I am only persuaded that the *meme* of the Blue Lady has reached immortality.

CHAPTER 3. THE TOWN

> "I mused for a few moments on the question of which was worse, to lead a life so boring that you are easily enchanted, or a life so full of stimulus that you are easily bored."
>
> —Bill Bryson

In contrast to the surrounding countryside and satellite communities, Nashville is anything but a ghost town. It is very much alive, and has a surprising number of amenities. There's a nice library, a YMCA, a sizable middle and high school which draws students from the whole county, a fine brewery, an astonishing four wine tasting rooms, and about 200 little shops, every last one of which sells caramel corn.

The Nashville Courthouse is the centerpiece of the village, looking a bit like a church itself, where there is but one elected judge who labors over a docket clogged with divorce and child support cases, and all too familiar recurring criminal matters (DWI, public intoxication, domestic battery and a host of drug-related offenses). It is there where you will find the county's only metal detector, and despite the prevalence of firearms and knives (everyone born in Brown County carries a pocket knife—it's the law), that metal detector has never been put to use.

At the municipal building about a block away, you can see sausages being made at bi-monthly meetings of the County Counsel and County Commissioners. That's where people go to bitch about the county's legendary potholes, and that's where the county's power brokers postpone any really important decisions for future meetings, *ad infinitum*. Meetings of the County Commissioners and Counsel always convene with a prayer. Little else happens after that.

The Liars' Benches of Nashville

17. "How big did you say that fish was?"

In Brown County, if you are not in some manner involved in a business which serves tourists, you are either retired, disabled, on welfare, commute to work somewhere else, or cook meth. Years ago, Helmsburg had a sock factory, but it burned down. I can understand how a sawmill/lumberyard could burn down, but I never knew that socks were so flammable. The Season's Hotel burned down in 2006, and the Nashville Opry three years later. Both of those were caused by arson.

If you want to rub elbows with locals in Brown County, take a trip to the Nashville post office. Tourists have no legitimate business there. For reasons which are unclear to me, the Nashville post office will not deliver mail in "town," requiring residents to hold a post office box. Perhaps, by making residents walk a short distance to retrieve an arm-load of unsolicited pizza coupons, and occasionally, a tax warrant, eviction notice or call to jury duty, the US Postal Service is attempting to reduce the incidence of Type II Diabetes. From what I can observe, if this was the intention, the program has had limited success.

An entire culture pervades the Nashville post office. It is a place to share gossip, exchange kind words with acquaintances you'd never want to invite into your home, or catch someone who's been avoiding your calls or service of process. The people running the post office are as inept and inefficient as postal workers anywhere else, but here at least they are friendly and know your name.

Occasionally, at the post office, you'll have an awkward encounter with someone you truly detest. Since the post office is neutral territory, it is an unspoken rule that you never draw your gun in these circumstances. That same chance meeting at the Pine Room could easily turn lethal.

At the post office, it's especially difficult when you must stand in line with someone you loathe. Local etiquette mandates that you make small talk. So, rather than asking "Gee, did your sister Jackie figure out that I'm not the daddy?," or "Did your son Jake ever get paroled?," conversation inevitably turns to the weather. In my view, this is analogous to the innocuous canine practice of butt-sniffing while on a short leash.

Nashville also has a fine hardware store, Bear Hardware. Locals simply say "Bear." "I need to go to Bear" means, "I have a need for an esoteric plumbing or electrical part, or perhaps bailing wire, so I intend to visit the local hardware store." If you need drywall screws, a Coleman stove, liquid propane, drill bits, a ¼ inch CPVC elbow, space heater, or a new pocket knife, go to Bear. Unlike Menards, which generally has lower prices enabling you to save big money, a real, live human being will assist you at Bear. Unlike the post office, there will be some tourists in Bear. But the vast majority of the people at Bear will be locals.

One of the most memorable experiences you'll have at Bear is olfactory. NPK fertilizers (i.e., those containing a combination of nitrogen, phosphorus and potassium—great for tomatoes) have a distinctive odor, and that odor permeates Bear. So does the aroma of popcorn dripping with trans-fats. Bear gives a free bag of popcorn to anyone who wants it. The smell of sawdust is notably absent, because Bear doesn't sell lumber. Go visit Bill Pool in Helmsburg for that.

Oddly enough, you can buy a lot of clothes at Bear, too. T-shirts with rebel flags, and stuff like that. Bear has a full line of Carhartts, and if you work outdoors in the winter, nothing beats a Carhartt. Also, if you need to bend over to fix a furnace or major appliance, the Carhartt makes the "plumber's crack" a thing of the past. Bear also has some redneck signs to decorate your man-cave, bearing such gems as: "I miss my wife, but my aim is improving!"

Years ago, someone wanted to put a Starbucks in Nashville, but the good citizens of Brown County set fire to the building and performed a public hanging of the wannabe baristas at the courthouse. Just kidding. But for almost a decade after the noisy remonstrators departed, a derelict building stood where the Starbucks was supposed to go. The residents here prefer a derelict building to a Starbucks. As I pen these words, that building has finally been repurposed into an ice cream shop, affiliated with the iconic "Chocolate Moose" in Bloomington. I hope they bought fire insurance.

Local remonstrators may be the reason why there are but two fast food restaurants in the whole county: a McDonald's and a Subway. Each is located within a tobacco-spit of one of Nashville's three traffic lights. So if you really have a craving for fast food, just look for a traffic light and park. There's a 2/3 chance that you'll find your gustatory treasure.

Nashville has three gas stations, too. They are indistinguishable from gas stations in any other small Kentuckiana town. Each is appended to a convenience store which offers the necessities of Kentuckiana life: milk, white bread, bagged ice, candy, gum, salted snacks, motor oil, radiator fluid, stale donuts, energy drinks, rolling papers, chewing tobacco, cigarettes, lottery tickets, and a host of inedible ready-to-go meals (the most provocative being the coquettishly-colored nitrite-soaked hot dogs which rotate on a spinning grill for weeks on end, waiting for just the right suitor to come along). At Kentuckiana convenience stores, you will find fountain drinks and slushies of gargantuan proportions, dispensed into polystyrene containers which, when empty, miraculously float away under their own power from the vehicle's dash board cup holder, and come to rest on the side of the road.

Relatively few Kentuckiana natives have credit cards, making payment at the pump problematical. Here you will see this oft-repeated ritual: a battered car or truck pulls up to a pump. The tattooed driver flicks his last butt onto the ground. With engine running and radio blaring, he enters the store, throws down a $20 bill for cigarettes and perhaps a Polar Pop and a lottery ticket, and then tells the clerk "I'll take the rest in gas." After lighting a new cigarette, he dispenses gas until it stops by itself, and then drives off to the sound of screaming rubber.

Not far from the post office is the 4-H Fairgrounds, a place that comes alive a few days per year when people gather to compare sows and heifers, eat caramel corn, and show their skill at riding dirt bikes. In the parking lot, you'll see a wide range of domestic pick-up trucks both new and old, all of which have been adorned with after-market parts and accessories. Some vehicles customized in this fashion cannot be accessed without a stepladder.

For the young people in Brown County, the County Fair is a place where you can meet both a future meal AND a future mate. At the steamy climax of the County Fair each July, the place is improbably packed with pimply adolescents, some already sprouting tattoos, and the air is thick with enticing pheromones. Chicken fried lard is the *amuse bouche.*

Fortunately, there are some truly civilized places to hang out in Nashville. One of those is the Big Woods Brewery, located just west of the Courthouse. Some local businesspeople opened the brewery in 2008, and business has been gushing ever since. The beer of greatest notoriety is the "Busted Knuckle," which is too dark for my buds on account of my German ancestry. (I prefer the "Six Foot Blonde," for reasons I'd rather not make public.)

Big Woods has grown so rapidly that it is more of a little empire, consisting of the original brewery/restaurant, and now, a pizza shop. The brewery itself was relocated to a converted bowling alley about a mile north of the town's center, when it ran out of capacity a few years ago. The brewery/bowling alley is open for imbibing, too. Being close to Bloomington, a college town, apparently hasn't hurt business.

You won't find many locals at Big Woods. That's because the locals only drink Budweiser or Bud Light. No, let's not yield to stereotypes. Some of the locals have been known drink Miller Lite on occasion, too. If you want to meet locals in the presence of alcohol, try the Pine Room. It's in a strip mall next to a Dollar General, near the McDonald's at one of the county's three traffic lights.

Nashville also has an astonishing four wine-tasting rooms. One is affiliated with Brown County Winery located in Gnaw Bone, just file miles east of Nashville. The owners, Dave and Cynthia Schrodt, have been bottling great wines there since the 1980s. From the looks of it, they're doing well, too. The tasting room sits right across the street from the Courthouse, to the south. It opens just about the time they're done doing arraignments at the Courthouse.

Another tasting room is a southern outpost of Chateau Thomas Winery in Plainfield, which is located north of the LGM. Its tasting room is but a stone's throw to the south, and you can stagger there by means of a back alley to avoid drawing the attention of the local constabulary (more of that later). The owner of the Chateau Thomas Winery, Charley Thomas, gave up his practice as an Obstetrician to give birth to fine Malbecs and Zinfandels. Some years back, Charlie hit a financial home run with a sweet pink wine fortified with Splenda. I advise you to stick with his Malbec.

Cedar Creek Winery and Salt Creek Winery have each established new tasting rooms in Nashville. Call for hours of operation—Nashville rolls up its sidewalks seasonally.

To the east of the Courthouse is the Brown County Historical Society, which has a treasure trove of local memorabilia. If you plan to visit Nashville, budget a couple of hours to do it justice. Just make sure they're open first. The hours are unpredictable, and sometimes, they're closed even when the sign says they're supposed to be open.

And, of course, there are about 200 little shops in Nashville, most of them only open when water may reliably be found in liquid form. The shops sell everything from candles to fudge, Harley Davidson leather jackets, prints by local artists, wood carvings, and nick-knacks that should never be caught in the possession of a heterosexual man.

If you detest shopping, as I do, and find yourself in the company of a woman who is irresistibly drawn to such things, there are several nice coffee shops where you can kill time, gossip or read. I recommend a place called

"Common Grounds," just a skip from the Big Woods Brewery. Speaking of coffee . . .

Slightly north of Nashville, in a place that does not welcome tourists, is a coffee roaster of considerable talent. Nick Schultz, a coffee geek, has been importing and roasting Arabica beans for a decade, and he confines his business to supplying Kentuckiana's finest restaurants. You can't get a cup of coffee directly from Nick, but you can get a cup of Nick's coffee at several places in Nashville as well as the Story Inn. Nick is related to Benjamin, and Cynthia Schultz.

A fine new county Jail sits across from the schools, a bit removed from the courthouse and 4-H Fairgrounds. There, a small department consisting of jack-booted thugs affiliated either with the Nashville Town Police or the Brown County Sheriff's Department are available to assure that it is nearly always filled to capacity. In Brown County, the cops do more than enforce the law. They ARE the law. And they know it.

Time for a rant.

The FBI keeps a lot of records on ordinary Americans, but amazingly, it does not keep a tally of how many of us are killed each year at the hands of our own police officers. A British newspaper, *The Guardian*, has an interactive website which largely fills this information void, and by its estimation, American cops kill at least 1,000 American citizens each year. That's far more Americans than died in foreign wars since 9/11. Chicago's cops alone gun down 50 citizens per year, on average. That's more killing than cops typically do in all of Europe, even with its restive Muslim population crammed into Stalin-esque barracks.

An American is 100 times more likely to be killed by a cop than is a European, and at least 29 times more likely to be killed by a cop than by a terrorist. And for those of you who think that the Second Amendment's right to bear arms gives pretext for cops to "defend" themselves, let it be known that an American citizen is 100 times more likely to be killed by a cop than the other way around.

First came the "War on Drugs," which brought us draconian sentencing guidelines passed by pandering politicians attempting to placate a petrified public. Then came the propitious attacks of 9/11, the "War on Terror" and the birth of the surveillance state.

Over the years, we've given cops free reign. Courts, prosecutors, and jurors accept their testimony, it seems, without question.

No one wants to be accused of being "soft on crime." I have personally witnessed three Brown County cops flat out lie in their police reports, on unrelated matters. Inasmuch as these were the only three criminal matters with which I have had any contact as a lawyer in this county for a decade, that's a pretty high percentage—100%—of fabrication.

We have become a nation of cop-enablers. And the cops know it. They stretch the truth. They fib. They actively provoke people under questioning. They tamper with evidence and yes, sometimes they torture and kill. And when one of them pulls a gun, you can bet that his comrades will circle the paddy wagons to protect him.

18. "No witnesses"

Do not expect our unimaginative politicians to make a change. Cop-enabling is a passion of both the right and the left. The left embraces the growth of government at all levels, including law enforcement (especially if they are unionized). The right eschews the growth of government, except when it comes to law enforcement (regardless if they are unionized). As Mark Twain said: "No country can be well governed unless its citizens as a body keep religiously before their minds that they are the guardians of the law, and that the law officers are only the machinery for its execution, nothing more." In this regard, we have failed.

There are some decent folks in local law enforcement, but the rotten apples put our local constabulary on par with the trigger-happy cops in Chicago and elsewhere. In 2013, two of Brown County's finest gunned down an unarmed man they were attempting to take into custody. His crime: a parole violation. The consequences for shooting him dead: none.

Deputy Rick Followell was once disciplined for sleeping in his patrol car during a night shift (here, like everywhere else, it's almost impossible to fire a cop). The voters of Brown County, who were obviously impressed with his laid-back attitude, then elected him sheriff. Upon his coronation, the new sheriff began posting mug shots on the department's official Facebook page, of people ARRESTED in Brown County, with a synopsis of what the cops claimed they were doing wrong.

A good number of these poor bastards were stopped and searched by police without so much as a scintilla of probable cause. (My favorite pretext for a Brown County stop and search was the suspect's temerity to make "eye contact" with the officer.) So much for the 4th Amendment and the time-honored notion that one is innocent until proven guilty.

Such public shaming of friends and kinfolk (almost everyone's related here, by blood or marriage) was even more than the gossip-hungry local voters could stomach, so Followell was booted from office in 2014, and his successor mercifully scrubbed these nasties from the department's Facebook page.

Our sister state Illinois (a state in which a majority of living former governors may now be counted among America's prison population) saw fit to make it a felony to record a police officer while making an arrest. In 2013, the Supreme Court sensibly let stand a Seventh Circuit case striking that law down as unconstitutional. Yes, you may now pick up your cell phone camera and record cops in the line of "duty."

Alas, your cell phone may be your best protection against these predators. Just don't waste the effort using it to call 911.

So if you ever find yourself in Brown County, beware of cops on the prowl. Each year, some five million tourists descend upon the county, to hike the trails, ride horses or mountain bikes, eat caramel corn, have sex, belly-laugh, and generally enjoy themselves. The presence of so many people with money in their pockets, without close kin in the county, has proved to be a temptation too great to resist.

If you leave a tavern or brewery after 11 pm and have an out-of-town license plate, just count on being pulled over and searched. The 4th Amendment does not apply. And if you quote the 4th Amendment to a cop in the line of "duty," you can easily lose your balance, fall against a curb, and have your teeth knocked out.

Fixing this obvious problem will require some serious changes to the status quo, not just in Brown County, but everywhere that cops have gone feral. At very least, we should equip all cops with body cameras, and all patrol cars with dash cams, neither of which can be tampered with or switched off at the discretion of a cop who's about to go in for the kill. It's the equivalent of putting a radio collar on a grizzly bear or other dangerous carnivore. Given cops' penchant for "losing" evidence that might incriminate them, those recordings should be entrusted to an independent third party and made available to any citizen who files a FOIA request.

If you drive a late model car, it will be equipped with a "black box" mandated by the US government. Your handy cell phone is a tracking device that is monitored by the NSA. Our government tracks us. But incredibly, though we record the movements of every law-abiding citizen, we give cops a pass.

In addition, before hiring a cop, perhaps we should administer an MMPI to at least screen out the sociopaths. Finally, and most radically, it should be possible to fire a cop for good cause. And killing someone without good cause should constitute "good cause" to fire someone, and written into any future union contract.

Radical stuff.

End of rant.

CHAPTER 4. THE CALL OF THE WILD

> "Animals are companions on this planet,
> not necessarily our feedbags."
>
> —D. A. Pennebaker

If you live in the country, as I do, you must own a dog. It's not the law, but it should be.

My best friend is Snow, a German Shepherd-farm dog mix that would have made Jack London proud. She was sired and born in Gatesville, about thirteen miles to the north of Story. Snow's a fixture on the Story Inn's front porch whenever she's not lathering me with affection, or pretending to hunt deer.

The country is no place for pugs, Pekingese or other toy breeds. In the country, you need a real dog.

As the name implies, German Shepherds were first bred in Germany. The English fell in love with the breed but had a more difficult time falling in love with Germans. Thus, for many years, they were known as "Alsatian Wolf-Dogs," which is a far more flattering name anyway. I would also commend the English for implicitly recognizing Alsace to be a part of Germany, not France.

As best as we can determine, humans first domesticated the wolf, *Canis lupis*, long before we gave up our hunting-gathering ways. Since people settled down in the Fertile Crescent a lot earlier than, say, in Brown County, the date of domestication is much debated. But very clearly, the dog has been our friend and companion for many, many years. Whether the point of domestication occurred once, or simultaneously in many places, or off and on in many places over many years, spanning many human civilizations, from different wolf varieties, will perhaps never be known. Suffice it to say, *Canis familiaris* and *Homo sapiens* have been co-evolving ever since.

It was a good fit. The dogs patrolled the village perimeter and accompanied the hunters on the hunt. Once the prey was wounded, the dogs would hound it (if you will pardon the pun) until either the slow-footed humans could catch up and dispatch it or it died of exhaustion. Regardless, the hunt was later followed by a campfire feast in which all ate their fill of protein.

As our village companions, dogs effectively improved humans' sense of hearing and smell by orders of magnitude. That's more than evolution could have done for us acting alone, and that added visual and auditory acuity surely would have come at a price, perhaps a smaller brain. The human brain accounts for about 2% of an adult's body mass, but it consumes about 20% of that person's calories and oxygen. It's an expensive organ, but obviously confers evolutionary benefits exceeding its cost. Otherwise, we wouldn't have it. Perhaps dogs vicariously gave us better hearing, eyesight and swiftness, enabling us to devote our time to making tools, campfires and eventually space ships. (Come to think of it, it was a dog, Laika, who was first to orbit the earth, in 1957.) We, in turn, have bequeathed dogs a hearth, a home, and (more recently) immunization from fleas, ticks, rabies, distemper and heartworms, not to speak of the chance to be the first mammal to orbit the earth. (Sadly, *Canis familiaris* has delegated its thinking to us and is a dullard compared to its wild kin.)

Late in the evening, after the kitchen is closed, I'll sometimes let Snow into the tavern. Nothing better evinces our co-evolution than to see numerous hands reach down to pet her. It's an irresistible human impulse. In return, Snow nearly faints with pleasure when she's shown that affection. A human life is simply incomplete without one of these noble creatures.

Snow's wolf ancestry is much in evidence. Her floppy puppy ears began to stand up straight, all by themselves, at an appropriately early age. She hardly ever barks. But she howls, especially if she hears coyotes in the distance. On one recent spring evening at Story, a customer's car alarm went off. Snow responded with howls. Amused tavern patrons, enjoying the warm weather outside, began howling too. The scene would have gone viral on the Internet had someone possessed the mental acuity to pull out a cell phone and record it.

Snow loves to travel with me in the car, and when she spies a herd of deer, she becomes riveted with attention. On such occasions, I sometimes indulge her predatory instincts by stopping and opening the door, in which case she'll blast off like a rocket, giving a full-hearted chase until she returns, exhausted and with tongue hanging, some minutes later. She and her little brother actually brought down a fawn together on Christmas Eve, 2015.

They returned with its dismembered body back to base camp, where I had a nice fire going. I declined their generous offer to share the bounty, but I must confess, I derived some vicarious Paleolithic pleasure in their behavior that evening.

This is not to say that human–dog evolution is complete. Dogs still display some unsavory behaviors like rolling in carrion and tackling garbage cans. But on balance, dogs bring us a great more benefits than embarrassments.

It is an undeniable fact that dogs LOVE us. Charles Darwin recognized the obvious, but we still had some behaviorists like BF Skinner deny the obvious as recently as the 1970s. Ridiculous.

Snow's ancestors prowled the hills of what would become Brown County at the LGM. When I take walks in the great forest near Story, Snow is always nearby, enthusiastically covering three times the distance, as I, in my bipedal way, gingerly step over logs and creeks in an effort not to fall on my ass or twist an ankle. We both love the great outdoors, and we love to enjoy it together. I often muse that Snow is sufficiently wolf-like to survive out there all by herself.

Frequently, I'll recreate the conditions of the first human–wolf encounter and build a large campfire. It is a time-honored tradition in Brown County to finish the night around a fire pit (locals pronounce it "far pee-it") drinking beer. It's human instinct to stare into the fire, probing it periodically to allow a flame to burst out. Snow's instincts command that she patrol the perimeter; you'll see her almost savage eyes glinting in the darkness. If there are coyotes yipping in the distance, she will answer with a mournful howl.

Wolves, coyotes and dogs can interbreed and produce fertile offspring, and in fact, in Brown County they do. Or at least dogs and coyotes interbreed, since there are no wild wolves here anymore. The resulting progeny, called coy-dogs, bear physical traits of each stock, and by dog standards, they are particularly skittish. Coyotes are fussy at picking partners and stick with respectable breeds like Dobermans and German Shepherds. They will spurn the amorous advances of a pug or Pekingese by killing and eating it.

The Indiana Department of Natural Resources is intent upon exterminating coy-dogs. Despite the DNR's best efforts, Kentuckiana's coyotes now carry more than a drop of blood from *Canis familiaris*. Old timers say the coyotes are bigger and bolder now than they were in the past. I have yet to see one approach the fire pit ("far pee-it").

A few years ago, we raised chickens here at the Story Inn. These were truly free-ranging and would wander among the patio guests demanding handouts, which most guests found to be amusing. At night, it was necessary to put them up into a coop. I sometimes had the chore of tucking the flock into bed, which occurred at dusk, no matter what time of year it happened to be. Chickens don't like to hang out at the fire pit after dark.

One evening, a raccoon found its way into the coop and killed several chickens. One of the servers at the restaurant heard the commotion and ended the carnage with the assistance of a .25 caliber pistol he just happened to be carrying in his pocket. (He also had a .22 caliber rifle in his car nearby, and had to make a split-second choice between these lethal instruments.) This guy is now a law student.

Unfortunately, the hens remembered the experience, and from that point on they refused to enter the coop at night. They took to roosting in a tree near the coop, some of them making a mess in the parking lot.

The local coyotes had a field day. Over the next several weeks, we lost a chicken every three or four days until the flock had been nearly exterminated. Nothing would be left but a few feathers. The killing always occurred at night, in stealthy silence.

After that experience, I didn't have the heart to bring the chickens back. We gave the remaining hens, as well as the henhouse, to some employee-friends who live down Elkinsville Road. There they keep company with hogs that are fattened almost exclusively with plate scrapings from the Story Inn's restaurant. To paraphrase Yogi Berra, it's ham and eggs, all over again.

19. Before the big fire.

Today, Brown County is about 80% forested, and the vast majority of that land is government-owned. The biggest chunk, by acreage, is the Hoosier National Forest. It extends, albeit in a fractured way, south all the way to the Ohio River. The other chunk is an impressive 16,000 acre state park, the largest in Indiana, known very cleverly as the Brown County State Park. Story shares a thousand-foot boundary with the park, and to the west and south, another boundary with the Hoosier National Forest as well as a soggy bottomland under the joint jurisdiction of the US Army Corps of Engineers and the Indiana Department of Natural Resources. This makes Story the connective tissue between three large contiguously forested tracts, and the largest canopy of hardwood forest to be found in the American Midwest.

What a privilege it is to be here.

20. From the ashes.

Before I became 90% deaf in the voice range (from an unfortunate bout of spinal meningitis as an adolescent, with the hearing loss becoming acute by my 50th birthday), it was truly a pleasure to hear the birdcalls and the rustling of branches in this forest. The place is quiet, but never silent. On one sunny spring afternoon years ago, Frank Mueller and I watched as a bald eagle soared over the General Store heading west, toward the lost town of Elkinsville. We were both silent—human speech could only have detracted from that moment.

It wasn't always this way. When white settlers arrived here, they saw an old-growth forest the likes of which had not been seen in Europe for 10,000 years. It didn't take them long to cut it all down.

Whereas the English logged the American eastern wilderness to build warships for the noble purpose of killing the French, the settlers of Indiana logged the land to build homes and towns to make room for more people, and then burned what was left to keep them warm until someone discovered that Indiana was blessed with bituminous coal as well. Photographs of the "old" General Store (it burned down in 1915, to be replaced a year later by the current "new" General Store) show the hillsides behind totally denuded of vegetation.

At about that time, this conversation occurred between two settlers, Bevis and Butthead:

Bevis: Uh, heh heh, man, the trees are GONE!

Butthead: Heh, heh, yeah. That really sucks.

Bevis: Well, uh, heh, heh, what are we gonna do now? Move west?

Butthead: Heh, heh, I donno. What are we gonna do?

Bevis: Well, uh, maybe we should do something different.

Butthead (smacking Bevis): Like what? Heh. Heh.

Bevis: Like, uh, maybe we can farm. Heh. Heh.

And that is how Brown County transitioned from being a logging community into an agricultural community.

It wasn't an easy transition. By logging the forest, the settlers removed the anchor to the topsoil, which unleashed an epic amount of erosion. Today, although the forest has recovered somewhat, the hilltop remains rather barren, a good deal of its soil having come to rest in the flat bottomlands. The flat bottomland is the only place in Brown County that can be profitably farmed today (without federal subsidies, that is—I feel another rant coming on).

Farming proved to be a marginal enterprise, the glacier having left Brown County unscathed and bereft of the fertile till that makes the rest of Indiana a breadbasket. Then the Great Depression hit, and commodity prices tanked. Farming went from bad to worse, and people in Brown County abandoned their farmsteads for greener pastures, which was almost anywhere else but Brown County. Between 1930 and 1940, the county lost half its population, in an exodus that must have been reminiscent of Steinbeck's *Grapes of Wrath*.

Farmland escheated to the government for non-payment of taxes, and in a moment of lucidity, it dawned upon a German immigrant and conservationist named Colonel Richard H. Lieber to turn the whole place into a park. In this manner, and with his powers of persuasion, the Indiana state park system was born.

The "New Deal" Democrats did their best to repair the damage from clear-cutting the forest, and through the newly-formed Civilian Conservation Corps, paid people who would otherwise have been unemployed to plant about one million new trees in Brown County. The CCC also built an impressive lodge in the newly-formed park, one which survives today. It's called the Abe Martin Lodge, after the legendary character created by cartoonist Kin Hubbard.

We have a rusty old CCC helmet in the tavern at Story, and it looks a bit like a WW-I issue helmet, except that it's tan instead of olive drab. Some of these people who built the park were black, and they had the good sense to leave after the project was completed. I get the impression that they didn't go out on the town much when they were here.

Unfortunately, the CCC planted the wrong trees, ones which were native to Canada, well above the LGM and better suited to a cooler climate. In this epoch, Brown County should not be a coniferous forest, and the Jack Pines quickly took root but then mostly died. Being adapted to shed dry snow from their needle-like leaves, they didn't do well in ice storms. At least they were fast-growing, completing their life cycle in about a century.

Today, one can still find groves of these non-native Jack Pines, fully mature and ready to fall on someone's house, garage or trailer. I personally had over 100 mature Jack pines logged from the Story property. A local farmer, Dean Manual, brought his portable sawmill to our property and cut them into boards and posts, which we deployed into making fences and paneling. We didn't have to visit Bill Pool for a while. If you visit the Old Mill or the Tavern at Story, you'll see at least three thousand board feet of paneling that was logged right here. It is clear that this is exactly what the CCC planners had in mind for the Jack Pines.

Meanwhile, the native hardwood species made a slow comeback, and except for the elm (killed by Dutch Elm Disease) and the ash (killed very recently by the Emerald Ash Borer), the old forest has returned. Today, we have most of the original species back, except that the clear-cutting but a century ago has skewed the age structure a bit. Imagine a large audience in which the oldest person is 30 years of age. It would look like a rally for Bernie Sanders, everyone sporting horned-rimmed glasses, day-old beards and knitted hats, and not one of them having the foggiest idea of what "socialism" really means.

The people who remained in Brown County and greater Kentuckiana were a tough lot and quickly discovered that they could add value to what little grain they could coax from the land by fermenting it. In this manner, the culture of moonshining was born, made all that more profitable by the propitious passage of the 18ᵗʰ Amendment which made illegal the "manufacture, sale or transportation of intoxicating liquors" within the United States. Very notably, as I edify my incredulous students, it was still perfectly legal to drink and drive a car during Prohibition.

Captured Still when (?anne ?anidleptly Sheriff.

21. "Boys, I don't want this to disappear from the evidence room!"

The moonshine culture is much in evidence today, anywhere you go in Kentuckiana. South of the Ohio River, you can find the world's best spirits, and the only true bourbon. North of the Ohio River, they're still perfecting the recipe. The art of clandestine manufacture of something that's illegal is now rooted in our DNA. We make the world's best methamphetamine in Kentuckiana, too, I am told.

Now I will rant.

As an 18ᵗʰ Century Liberal, I am loath to condemn anything that people can do to themselves that doesn't hurt anyone else. That includes dope-smoking. From what I can tell, dope has wonderful potential as a pain reliever, and as my sister-in-law battles bone cancer, I have to believe that there is some good that can come if it. My only observation is that prolonged, heavy dope usage robs people of ambition and makes them stupid. A good number of them vote reflexively for Democrats. Whether that's a cause or an effect of dope usage is a matter for further debate.

While cannabis has medicinal properties, there are no redeeming qualities to meth, aside from the fact that occasionally someone raises property values around here when he burns his trailer to the ground while attempting to cook up a batch. In 18 years, I've had hundreds of employees come and go through the Story Inn, and as the hospitality business goes, that's about the average rate of turnover for a business of this size. Turnover is common. So is drug use.

During that time, I have come to recognize meth users. I can spot them from a mile away. They simultaneously exude an air of truculence and a pall of death, and until the inevitable overdose which puts them underground, they will steal you blind to get a fix. I stopped trying to save the world by rehabilitating them. If you're skinny, tweak and irascible, have bad teeth, and refuse to take a urine test, I show them the door. Our local dentist (there's only one in the whole county—his name is Steven Junken) has also become an expert at spotting meth use.

Hitler apparently used meth to energize his troops to fight Russians. If you can't get a warm meal to them at Stalingrad, then meth is the next best thing. That worked great for Hitler, because none of those troops came home.

People high on meth believe themselves to be invincible. In that respect, meth is a lot like cocaine. When people smoke dope, they want to eat Kit Kats and marvel at the hidden meanings behind shampoo commercials. On cocaine, you want to have sex for hours on end (so I'm told). Performance anxiety is not an issue.

When you're on meth, you feel like killing people. Sometimes, you do.

Four years ago, after I had retired for the evening with the woman who was soon to be my third ex-wife, my son Rich woke me up to inform me that a bar patron was "making trouble." To my everlasting chagrin, I leapt to the conclusion that he'd been over served and believed that I could calm him down, Gandhi-like, by offering him a free room and breakfast. When I approached him, with a body posture that would have calmed a rabid pit bull, he attacked me, dislocating my right shoulder and severing the subscapularis tendon. After rotator cuff surgery and six months of physical rehabilitation, I was able to get 90% of my range of motion back.

That's how I'll go to my grave, along with two titanium pins which are spotted by the ever-vigilant TSA-Gestapo whenever I attempt to board an airplane.

End of rant.

CHAPTER 5. THE WINES: BLESSINGS FROM THE PONTIFF

> "In vino veritas" ("In wine there is truth")
>
> —Pliny the Elder

When people think of Kentuckiana, wine is not ordinarily the first thing that comes to mind. It should be.

When European immigrants poured into Kentuckiana over the Ohio River, they immediately recognized it to be a natural grape growing region. It is no accident that the world's greatest wine grape regions can be found along the mighty rivers of Europe.

In 1802, Swiss immigrants founded the country's first winery in Vevay, in southeast Indiana on the banks of the Ohio. To this day, the good people of Vevay celebrate the "Swiss Wine Festival" each summer.

For almost two decades, the Story Inn has been hosting the Indiana Wine Fair, a spring gathering which has grown to become one of the largest wine events in the Midwest. It was the brainchild of yours truly and Dr. Allen Dale ("Ole") Olson a/k/a the "Pontiff of Palate," and his wife Joan.

Ole and Joan developed a palate for fine wines while they lived in Europe, as cold war diplomats (that's where Ole's resemblance to the James Bond character ends). Joan trained at *La Varenne Ecole de Cuisine* in Paris and later befriended the late Julia Child. Ole's opinion about wine is so good that we've declared him to be infallible. That's how he came by the Pontifical salutation. Periodically, Ole will issue a Papal "Bull" about something viniferous, which we may never call into question.

We jointly came up with some ideas (some good, some not so good) over "lunch," while enjoying some of their trophy wines (always good). Those included a 1986 vintage Cuvée Dom Perignon (yes, sparkling wines will travel), and a magnum of 1970 Chateau Latour Pauillac (yes, we finished it, even the unfiltered dregs). We now display The Pontiff's empty chalices in a dining room at Story, which we've named "*Olsons Weinstube*" out of gratitude.

Ole continues to write a monthly wine newsletter for us, which is called "Sheer Lunacy" because it is published at the full moon. Through these efforts, The Pontiff does us the additional service of keeping earth's satellite safely in orbit.

The first lesson of wine tasting is this: if you like it, then it is good. Don't let the snobs tell you what you like.

The second lesson of wine tasting is this: decant the wine only if you want to impress your guests with the decanter. The wine will open by itself in the glass just fine.

The third lesson of wine tasting is this: don't waste a lot of money on the glass. Currently, Riedel stemware is all the rage. But it's designed to shatter into a thousand pieces with a hearty toast. Instead, get a nice big globe at a discount place for 99 cents.

The fourth lesson of wine-tasting is this: there's nothing wrong with a screw cap. Screw caps are a technological improvement over natural corks; only snobs show distain for them.

The fifth lesson in wine tasting is this: If the wine comes with a cork, don't pick it up and sniff it. Real oenophiles will immediately think you're a novice. (It's like kicking a tire at a used car dealership.) Instead, gently squeeze the cork to make sure it did its job of keeping oxygen out of the bottle. If it doesn't break apart, the wine is probably OK.

Since the launch of the Indiana Wine Fair, Indiana's wines have improved markedly, according to a pontifical "Bull" from Ole that we may not call into question. Though they still pose little threat to the great houses of Bordeaux or Burgundy, Hoosier wines have gotten good enough to humble the cruelest wine snobs. I often do blind tastings with the best offerings; an acute palate will often open a closed mind. Diplomats should be forced to drink wine together.

We invite every Indiana winery to participate. Virtually all of the big ones do. Indiana now has upwards of 70 wineries; however, many of these are so small that they cannot effectively participate in the Wine Fair. On average, 30 or so wineries will make the trek to Story, and by volume, they represent over 90% of the wine production in the state.

The level of public interest is astonishing. Somehow, we'll cram 6,000 oenophiles into this little town to indulge in one-ounce complimentary samples of Rieslings, Malbecs and Cabernets. The wineries make a lot of money selling bottles to replenish wine cellars, which guarantees that they'll enthusiastically return in future years.

Story, for all of its remoteness, is actually the geographic center of Indiana's wine industry. The wineries like the Wine Fair for the additional reason that is doesn't involve a lot of travel.

As you can imagine, hosting an event of this size poses logistical challenges. We rent a 30-acre field from a local farmer for parking, and provide shuttle busses from Nashville. The event fills every hotel room in Brown County and in neighboring Bartholomew County as well. We pray to Jesus to provide loaves and fishes to feed them all, and to keep away the rain. We've never beseeched Christ for the additional miracle of turning water into wine, because the wineries always come well-stocked.

As Martin Luther said,

(I)f the devil should say, 'Do not drink,' you should reply to him, 'On this very account, because you forbid it, I shall drink, and what is more, I shall drink a generous amount. Thus one must always do the opposite of that which Satan prohibits. What do you think is my reason for drinking wine undiluted, talking freely, and eating more often, if it is not to torment and vex the devil who made up his mind to torment and vex me.'

Mercifully, wine festival-goers are a civilized lot, imbibe in moderation, and do not cause trouble.

In 2013, a 4,800 square mile area comprising the formidable chunk of Kentuckiana became recognized as an "American Viticultural Area" or AVA. It is known as the "Indiana Uplands AVA," for the simple reason that the Wisconsinan glacier left the landscape between Brown County and the Ohio River unscarred, and of higher elevation, than the surrounding terrain.

Within the AVA exist a wide variety of microclimates made possible by sloping terrain, bottomlands shielded from frost and wind, and, of course, proximity to the Ohio River. The soil, too, varies within the AVA, but limestone dominates in the south, providing alkalinity and decent drainage (Karst topography typically gives birth to "sink holes" and underground rivers, clearing the surface of water quickly). Overall, it's an interesting terroir. Currently, the AVA contains 17 wineries and 19 vineyards, with more acreage being planted every year.

Kentuckiana summers are hot, humid and buggy, requiring diligence in cultivating grapes. Historically, vintners have planted hybrids, like Chardonnel and Chambourcin, due to their hearty nature. More recently, winemakers have cautiously planted Pinot Noir, Cabernet Sauvignon, Malbec, Cabernet Franc, Sauvignon Blanc, Chardonnay, Riesling, Tennant, Petite Verdot and even Blaufrankish, with success. The traditional pure varietals are like trophy wives. They're high maintenance (and prone to hybridization if you turn your back).

I visited Turtle Run Winery recently and received an education from owner/winemaker Jim Pfeiffer. Jim is adamant that one must never add sugar to wines, something he equates to doping Olympic athletes. Yeast, it seems, prefers either glucose and sucrose to fructose, and will work their magic on fructose only as a last resort. Jim's been doing some interesting things by arresting barrel fermentation and then re-starting it.

Recently, Jim lost several acres of newly-planted pinot noir to a freakish cold snap. The loss did not dampen either his commitment to, or enthusiasm for, his project. We toasted the loss by opening his last bottle of pinot noir which, I will say, was remarkable (funeral dirge playing).

Turtle Run offers a nice blended dry white known as "The Spectrum," consisting of Sauvignon blanc, Chardonnay and Chenin blanc from a "re-roasted" barrel (Jim explained the process of re-roasting a barrel). I particularly liked his 2014 Cabernet franc which, despite being unblended, had layers and complexity. Here was both talent and terroir at work.

Jim is unconventional, to say the least. He likes to use blue bottles for his red wines (albeit in a traditional red wine bottle shape) because they are slightly better at screening out ultraviolet light. As a traditionalist, I struggled to get past the blue to really enjoy the red, always expecting a Riesling to pop out like a genie. Brad Cox, a talented local artist who built our tavern bar stools, makes beautiful bottle trees out of Turtle Run's unusual blue bottles.

About a 20-minute drive from Turtle Run is Huber Winery, where every morsel of fermented fruit is estate grown. The Huber family has been farming this land for over 150 years and quickly mastered the challenge of growing a wide variety of traditional European grape varietals. Their dry red blends are the best the Hoosier state has to offer. The "Heritage" is a mouthful of Cabernet Franc, Cabernet Sauvignon, Tannat, and Petit Verdot. The 2010 Heritage Reserve would compare favorably to any Bordeaux, in my opinion. Huber has a distillery, too (I generally eschew distilled beverages; my wine software ceases to function).

The extended Huber family has occupied and farmed a hilltop near Borden/Starlight for a very long time, and as entrepreneurs they must cater to the church bus crowd from Louisville and nearby communities. But if you are hungry after sampling wines, you might want to avoid Joe Huber's Family Farm & Restaurant. The place oozes wholesomeness, with families linking hands in mealtime prayer as if they were modeling for a Norman Rockwell painting. Joe Huber's actually serves some of the better Huber wines by the glass. It would be a fine place to visit, observe, drink and eat, were it not for the eats.

Despite the claim "country cooking from scratch," Jane and I only saw evidence of mass production. My "country pit ham" was processed, replete with the rind intact. It's a travesty to serve processed ham so close to Kentuckiana's "Ham Belt." Jane ordered the chicken livers, which were obviously breaded and bagged at a processing plant somewhere, and had the texture, and flavor, of an old tire. Jesus himself could not have made them edible. We bagged them up for the dog, but then thought better of it.

Winzerwald Winery specializes in traditional German white grape varietals which, despite my ancestry, I will consume only on occasion. Their vineyard sits very close to the Ohio River, and is obviously influenced by it. They make a traditional Gewürztraminer that is indistinguishable from the ones I've sipped in the Mosel region. (I despise Gewürtztraminer, but this was like coming home to momma's meatloaf, which I didn't like much, either.) Olfactory is closely connected to the memory centers of the brain, which is why we'll say we like something that we really don't like. Kudos to Winzerwald, despite my unfounded prejudices. They're the real deal.

To the west of Story, also in the Uplands AVA, is Oliver Winery, the oldest and by far the largest in Indiana. Oliver has a lot of grapes under cultivation, but due to its sheer size, must still buy grapes from Lodi and Napa. Oliver markets its AVA fruit under its "Creekbend" label.

If you have the good fortune to visit Oliver's fine tasting room north of Bloomington, start off with the 2014 "Creekbend III," a complex blend of estate-grown whites that linger on the tongue. Among reds, start with the 2014 Corot Noir, a light, delightfully fruit-forward wine. The 2014 Creekbend Chambourcin is lovely, too, but a bit tannic. Their best estate-grown wine is the 2013 cabernet sauvignon, or so I am told. Oliver produced only 73 cases, and I did not have the opportunity to taste it. Owner Bill Oliver apparently guards these with the conviction of a she-bear protecting her cubs, and Bill was out of the office when I visited most recently.

Not far from Oliver is Butler Winery, which has a nice tasting room with a pastoral view (Oliver is located on a highway, and there's a bit of road noise). Owner Jim Butler briefly served with me on the Indiana Tourism Council, and his dedication to viticulture is much in evidence. Go there on a warm day, and enjoy a glass of 2014 Norton while sitting on the back deck. You won't find the 2013 Cabernet Sauvignon, because it's sold out.

I've visited every one of the Upland AVA wineries, and make an effort to re-visit four or five of them each year. When a new one opens, like Salt Creek Winery near Freetown, I'll beat a path to their door.

Adrian and Nicole Lee, the owners of Salt Creek, are now regular customers at the Story Inn's tavern. Recently, I had the honor of sampling their new cabernet sauvignon, bottled that very day. It had a metallic nose that dissipated almost immediately after opening. The wine paired beautifully with soft cheeses. (Interestingly, Adrian and Nicole prefer to drink local micro-beers while away from the winery.)

One AVA winery that I visit most often is Brown County Winery, because it's just ten miles from Story. We've got two of their wines on our list, a Catawba and a Port. They have two dry reds, a Merlot and a Cabernet Sauvignon, which are quite tasty. Unfortunately, at the present time, neither of those were grown in the AVA.

As the Ohio River snakes its way from Cincinnati to Louisville, past Vevay, Madison and dozens of villages, there are several wineries to see, and all worth the effort. No visit to Kentuckiana is complete without a trip to a half-dozen or more wineries, and an overnight stay at a bed & breakfast in Madison.

Pack aspirin, and watch out for cops.

CHAPTER 6. THE POLITICS.

> "Nobuddy can talk as interestin' as th'
> feller that's not hampered by facts er informa-
> tion."

—Abe Martin

Politics in Brown County is just as vacuous as it is everywhere else. Former House Speaker Thomas Philip ("Tip") O'Neill is attributed with saying "All politics is local," and in that respect, Brown County may serve as Exhibit A.

Like everywhere else, there are two political parties in America's benighted flyover middle. And those political parties have rigged the game to assure that we'll never live long enough to see the emergence of a third political party to challenge that duopoly.

In the absence of competition, there's not much of an incentive to please your customers. I learned that while on a swimming trip to a city then called Leningrad, before the collapse of the old Soviet Union. I had a pocket full of Rubles, but there was nothing worthwhile to buy. (I cruelly took to throwing the Rubles on the street and watching people dive for them.) In this country, we have two parties instead of one, but both are consumed with perpetuating their own power, not in providing sensible governance. Just look at the options we had for President this past election cycle.

Democrats and Republicans occur in about equal numbers in Brown County. But it wasn't always that way. As recently as the Carter Administration, Republicans were as scarce as black people. Changing demographics and trends in the national Democratic Party itself began to shift that balance toward Republicans, starting about 1980.

Quite a number of retirees began moving to Brown County, and they tend to be old, white, have money, and reflexively vote Republican. More recently, meth and heroin usage began to kill off a lot of the younger Democrats, and quite often, felony convictions have rendered a good number of those remaining alive ineligible to vote. The election of America's first black president in 2008 did not sit well with many local Democrats, who jumped ship. Even more jumped ship in 2016, when a New York billionaire with a fondness for flattery and gold-plated bathroom fixtures bamboozled them into believing that he was just another one of the boys. When you live in America's forgotten flyover middle, you'll jump at anything that smacks of empowerment.

Jane Ammeson was so distraught by the Trump victory that she immediately took a week off in Mexico. She wanted to see the place one last time, before the wall went up. The University of Pennsylvania had to bring in puppies and coloring books to console bereaved students who were not so mobile.

Suffice it to say, prior to 1980 Brown County effectively had only one political party, and now it has two.

If America has any homogeneity left, you will find it in the GOP, and Brown County is no exception. In Brown County, Republicans are all white, middle aged, middle class, members of a Christian church somewhere, and invariably members of either the Lions or Rotary Clubs. They mostly drive SUVs with stick families pasted on the back window. They love cops and suffer from the delusion that cops are there to protect them.

However, Republicans here, and elsewhere in Kentuckiana, have acquired characteristics which subtly distinguish them from their boring suburban counterparts from Ohiana and places to the east that are even more sophisticated. That's why I call them "Redneck Reds." "Redneck Reds" drive late-model pick-up trucks as well as SUVs. Both kinds of vehicles have stick families pasted on the back window. They often choose to home-school their children, and if they send them to school, they will lobby for a science curriculum in which intelligent design shares equal time with evolution. They overwhelmingly deny the existence of climate change, and they pray a lot. My Redneck Red friends take mild offence to being invited to the Story Inn's "Appropriate rural nondenominational open house and holiday party, clothing required," and not to its "Christmas Party."

You are a Kentuckiana "Redneck Red" if:

1. You think stem cells are human beings.
2. You own a Dixie Chopper.

3. You believe that "climate change" is a hoax cooked up by "Royal Blues" in order to scare us into building solar and wind farms at taxpayer expense.

4. You think that government should stay out of our lives, except that it is OK for the government to dictate to us how we may lawfully employ our own reproductive organs.

5. You think that "real Americans" look and act like the people you see in Norman Rockwell paintings.

6. You think homosexuality is a mental illness that can be cured with therapy and prayer.

7. You think that having a "strong national defense" requires us to spend more money than the next seven countries behind us combined, even when five of those countries are allied with us.

8. You think the Constitution entitles you to carry an Uzi into a grade school.

9. You have a secret stash of gold bars, ammunition, water bottles and canned goods.

10. You support the death penalty . . . for illegal aliens.

11. You visited the Creation Museum in Petersburg, Kentucky, on your way to your vacation in Pigeon Forge.

12. You believe that God loves and protects Christians . . . especially the Israelis.

13. You fear that our benevolent God will punish us if we pray to him at home instead of at school.

14. You think ketchup is a vegetable.

15. When people refer to our former president as a "Keynesian," you think they are referring to his place of birth.

The Democrats in Brown County are all white, too. But they are starkly divided into two camps that bear little resemblance to each other, except for the fact that both groups smoke dope.

Until about 1980, the County's old-line families were all Democrats, and they controlled local government as thoroughly as Tammany Hall controlled New York, or Dick Daley ruled Chicago. They had a powerful leader in Andy Rogers, a visionary businessman who turned Nashville into the tourist trap that it is today. Andy co-opted the local Democrat party as thoroughly as any political boss of that era. At various times, he sat on every appointed board in the county, and influenced the selection of everyone else who sat on those boards with him. To my knowledge, Andy Rogers never held an elected office of his own.

But these old-family Democrats were nothing like the imperious coastal liberals we've come to associate with the Democrat party today. The locals were first cousins to the now extinct "Dixiecrats" south of the LGM, the ones who opposed the Civil Rights Act of 1964. If there had been black people in Brown County, the old-line Democrats would have been Klansmen, or at least segregationists. Think of George Wallace, and you get the picture.

I call this group the "Bruised Blues," because these people, rightly or wrongly, believe themselves to be ignored, even abused, by the national Democratic leadership. Bruises are purple. Continued irritation can lead to rashes, and rashes are red.

Bruised Blues used to reflexively vote Democrat, but Donald Trump changed that. Time will tell whether this crack in the "Blue Firewall" was merely an aberration, or something more permanent.

Bruised Blues tend to work (if they work at all), in the service industry, fly Dixie flags, watch NASCAR and Jerry Springer, and live in manufactured homes with lots of dogs chained up out back. Every last one of them smokes cigarettes.

Very few Bruised Blues have bank accounts, and if for some reason money passes through their hands, they quickly rush out and get another tattoo. Every one of them owns at least three vehicles, which they proudly display in their front yards, none of which is insured or runs reliably. Every Bruised Blue owns several guns, and celebrates the opening of hunting season with the same reverence that a Redneck Red celebrates Easter. They don't have any position with respect to climate change because they don't read enough to know what it is.

Frequently, Bruised Blues have family that's still ensconced in local office, and having kin in office is a game-changer, bringing them out in droves. Like politicians everywhere, the ones in Brown County pamper themselves with perks. Health and pension benefits are the driving force behind local politics, and, it seems, always will be.

You are a Kentuckiana "Bruised Blue" if:

1. Your daddy was a "Blue."

2. The union told you to vote "Blue."

3. You think government should tax only rich people, and leave cigarettes, gasoline and alcohol off limits.

4. You are dead; you rise from the dead on the second Tuesday of November in even-numbered years.

5. You drink at least one 32-ounce "Polar Pop" every day.

6. You are angry with "Wall Street" but cannot articulate why.

7. You were indignant when the bank repossessed your car.

8. You consider yourself a patriot, yet fly a Dixie flag in front of your house.

9. You were angry that you had to start looking for a job after collecting 90 weeks of unemployment compensation.

10. You think liposuction ought to be covered by Medicaid.

11. You think you can save for your retirement by buying lottery tickets.

12. You hate the richest "one percent" because they got that way by exploiting people like you.

13. You often shoot your guns at road signs.

14. You get angry at "big oil" when the price of gasoline goes up.

15. You think that someone else should pick up your trash.

The other species of Kentuckiana Democrat are Mother Jones versions of the imperious snobs we've come to associate with Democrats on either coast. Locally, they are dominated by PhD's from nearby Bloomington, artists, and greying Hippies. I call this group the "Royal Blues."

Royal Blues smoke marijuana, but never tobacco. They live in wooded tracts of five acres or more, in rustic homes that are clean and well furnished with books which decry society's injustices. They drive Volts or Priuses, read the Huffington Post online, favor abortion but oppose capital punishment, and believe that the denial of climate change is tantamount to a crime against humanity. Royal Blues are the only people in Kentuckiana who do not own guns. Royal Blues never, ever, break bread with Bruised Blues.

You are a Kentuckiana "Royal Blue" if:

1. You are a current or retired college professor or administrator, artist, or a member of the media; you have a pony tail and drink Chardonnay.

2. You think that being awarded an Oscar, Grammy or Emmy entitles one to speak authoritatively about poverty, green energy and world peace.

3. You believe that social ills can be fixed with social engineering dictated by "Royal Blues."

4. You think that a government dominated by "Royal Blues" is better positioned to spend your money for your benefit than you are.

5. You think it is easier to become a billionaire than it is to earn a PhD in Sociology.

6. You think that the government can create jobs by taking money away from the people who hire and giving that money to people who don't want to work.

7. You think that it is unfair to require public employees to save for their own retirement.

8. You think that bad schools can be fixed by giving more money to the teacher's union.

9. You think that Constitutional rights and government benefits should flow to groups and not to individuals.

10. You think it is the exclusive province of "Royal Blues" to call other people "racist."

11. You think it is "racist" to require that people show personal identification before voting.

12. You think that it is "racist" to suggest that we have completely objective, merit-based standards for admitting students to study at professional schools.

13. You love jobs, but you hate employers.

14. You hate the military, and you hate hydrocarbons.

15. You have a bumper sticker on your Toyota Prius or Chevy Volt which reads: "Coexist."

The daunting task of selecting leaders in Brown County, as well as in other places in Kentuckiana, begins with cordial meetings and discussions. Such discussions must originate in a tavern somewhere. It's the law in Kentuckiana.

At the Story Inn, village elders convene each Friday to solve local, national and global problems. Currently, the village elder with senior status is Dean ("Dino") Walls, a retired iron worker. It is an unspoken rule that no one takes Dino's seat at the end of the bar on Friday evenings. (Germans may recognize this as the "*Stammtisch*".) By closing time, all of the world's problems have been solved.

Unfortunately, no one remembers anything the next day. That's why it's necessary for the "Old Men" to meet regularly. (Editor's Note: Women are welcome at the "Old Men's Club," as long as they don't mind being referred to as "Old Men"; the only requirement for being an "Old Man" is to have reached your 50th birthday.)

Dino, like most Kentuckiana natives, pronounce "dog" as "dow-ga" and "old" as "ode." Dino doesn't mind a bit if I invite my "dow-ga" Snow into the "Old Man's Club."

On November 8, 2016, a political super volcano erupted in Kentuckiana and elsewhere, sweeping Donald Trump into the highest office of the land, and dragging not a few conservative partisans along with him. Trump's victory came as a complete surprise to the network talking heads, so-called Political "Scientists" at our blue-blooded, cocooned universities, and high-priced pollsters and political consultants. That's because none of them bothered to visit Dino in the Story Inn's tavern on any Friday night in the year before the election. Back when there were 16 candidates for the Republican nomination, and two for the Democratic nomination, we actually polled the village elders. They predicted a Trump victory. Bernie Sanders came in second. I kid you not.

It is fashionable, if not mandatory, for coastal people to be dismissive of America's flyover middle. For many, a visit to the heartland consists of a two-hour layover in Indianapolis or Cincinnati, where they spend almost all of their time attempting to reconnect to the Internet and having a stroke if they do not. To the people who live here, this smacks of arrogance. It didn't help things when the *Huffington Post* in its predictably snarky way began to cover the Trump campaign on its entertainment page. That garnered belly-laughs in San Francisco, but it gave heartburn to people in the heartland.

In my modest opinion, the biggest error of our political elites was to see our country as an amalgamation of groups of people—women, blacks, gays, Catholics, Jews, atheists, millennials, university graduates, Asians, Hispanics—and not as one country with distinctive cultural regions. They assume that these groups behave the same regardless of where they happen to live. The know-it-alls would then lay a map of such groups on top of that the artificial grid of state boundaries that we inherited from the days of America's westward expansion.

Royal Blues grudgingly admit that America is mostly white and Christian, but they tend to dismiss America's white Christian population as something akin to background noise, to be split up by wooing votes away with occasional appeals to white women, public employees, the working poor, and members of labor unions. From that point, the "experts" would calculate votes within each state based upon how each such demographic group was assumed to behave, and then solve the math. If one looks at America this way, it should be turning Blue. But it is not.

People like Dino see things very differently. If one could take a hack saw and carve off 50 miles of land facing the Atlantic and Pacific oceans, as well as a 50 mile swath of land around the southern tip of Lake Michigan beginning at Milwaukee and ending at Jane Ammeson's condominium in St. Joseph, Michigan, you would have a country that should be called "Land of the Blue." The rest of it is America.

Thus, from a bar stool in Kentuckiana and other places in America, it looks like the political elites are pandering to everyone but them. It doesn't sit well with people like Dino to be dismissed as irrelevant background noise.

Shortly before the election, I attended a Brown County barbeque replete with a bonfire, kegs of domestic beer, free-roaming kids and dogs, and live Bluegrass music. Trump supporters overwhelmingly dominated this crowd. But this was the wedding reception for Britani Williams and Dani Ham, two women whose ceremony I had officiated earlier, and the event was attended by a great many of their gay friends. According to the coastal political elites, this was not supposed to happen.

It should therefore come as no surprise that there were insurgencies in each political party. The party insiders decreed a long time ago that this was to be another tired Bush–Clinton re-run, but America would have nothing of it. Trump won; Bernie Sanders did not. (Sanders won the primary elections in many so-called "Red" states, including Indiana. People in America prefer "right" or "left" to "inside".)

Sanders did a lot of damage to Clinton in the process of losing, and the kiss-and-make-up between them at the Democratic Convention looked contrived. Clinton could not get rid of the allegations that she had rigged the Super Delegates. And then the smarmy Clintons predictably brought with them their signature scandals. For people like Dino, the process looked to be rigged, and the Clintons to be nothing more than well-connected crooks who were making another power grab with the complicity of their media allies. It didn't help to be labeled a "deplorable," either.

This, in a nutshell, is why we have a Trump presidency.

Let's talk about Rebel flags, briefly. As you cross the LGM on your way south, you'll see a good number of them. When you get past Frenchy's Pub in Morgantown, you'll see one in front of a mobile home in Bean Blossom, just a few miles further on. As you travel further south, you'll see a lot more of them, mostly in front of homes and fluttering behind old pick-up trucks. Sometimes, people wear t-shirts or head-scarves with the Rebel flag. You see a lot of them on Kentuckiana bumpers.

Bruised Blues display the vast majority of Rebel flags, and they mostly vote, or at least they mostly did vote, for Democrats. Royal Blues do not fly flags of any kind, save for the rainbow variety. Redneck Reds will occasionally display them, but that mostly ends at puberty. You are much more likely to see an anti-abortion sticker on a Redneck Red's vehicle than a Rebel flag.

I spent three interminable years in the deep south in the early 1980's, and I saw fewer of them there than I see in Kentuckiana these days. (Admittedly, in law school I spent more time with Brooklyn Jews than I did among North Carolina Klansmen.) The northern part of Kentuckiana, of course, fought for the Union. The south was putatively neutral. One may presume that the Rebel flag does not signify a serious desire to succeed from the Union and reinstitute slavery.

Periodically, we host Civil War "re-enactments" here at the Story Inn. Perfectly respectable people dress up in either Union or Rebel uniforms, and pretend to kill each other. They meet amiably for breakfast before the "battle", and jocularly afterward in the tavern after the "battle". There are no racists among these people, as far as I can tell. But, then again, I am not a Progressive like Jane Ammeson, so I would not be able to identify a "racist" if I saw one.

So what does a Rebel flag really symbolize in Kentuckiana?

I have asked that question of many customers in the Story Inn's tavern, in the most politically neutral voice I can muster. I am not easily confused for being black, so perhaps I am not the right person to ask that question in the first place. But I have asked it nevertheless.

I have always gotten the same answer, and it has come in this iteration: "Because I can". That begs a further question, "Why do you want to?"

Herein lies the nuance. When people lack power, they get angry. Every one of these Rebel flag fans is patriotic. They fly American flags, too. A disproportionate number of them have served in the armed forces. They are not rebels, or revolutionaries. But they are angry.

They are angry because they are poor and disenfranchised. Life seems not as good for them as it used to be, and in this respect, they are correct. Life expectancy in Kentuckiana is declining, as are most indices of health and prosperity. Some Rebel flag-flying Kentuckianans do resent minorities and immigrants, who they feel have been granted favored status. But relatively few of those are overtly racist, as best as I can tell, not being a Progressive like Jane Ammeson with the unique ability to detect such things.

The Democrat party, traditionally the party of labor unions and the working poor, has been co-opted by people with degrees from Harvard, Yale and Duke, who eat arugula and don't speak their language. Or worse, the Democrat party power-brokers have adopted a dismissive attitude and patronizing tone with their former clients. When you fill the freezer with locally-harvested venison each fall and heat your home in winter with wood you've chopped yourself, you do not want to hear an east coast Progressive's lecture about the health hazards of high fructose corn syrup. Flying a Rebel flag is a bit like acting out an aggression without actually breaking the expensive china.

This, in a nutshell, is why people fly Rebel flags in Kentuckiana.

I cannot speculate as to how this phenomenon will play itself out in the years to come. Donald Trump resonates with many Bruised Blues. In 1980, while a law student at Duke, I saw the south improbably turn away from a Georgia peanut farmer and embrace a California movie actor. Before that, the Old South was deep Blue. In the years that followed, the Old South stayed Blue locally, but voted Red in national elections. But the Reds steadily gained ground, and by 2010 the south was effectively all Red, except for university town enclaves like Raleigh, Durham and Chapel Hill.

Or, more accurately and troublingly, in the Old South the whites are now Reds but the blacks are still Blues, the latter joined by a few Royal Blues and university snobs. I've been tempted to contact IU and demand a refund of the tuition I paid to get my Master's Degree in Political Science. Nothing has happened the way it was supposed to happen. If Trumpism proves to be more than aberration, and whites in America's flyover middle flee the Democrat party for good, it does not portend a rosy future for Democrats, or America.

Now that the dust has settled on the latest national election, discussion at the "Old Man's Club" has shifted to matters of more local, and mundane, concern.

As an unincorporated town, Story has no government. Each year since 1999, however, those same village elders have met on April 1 to elect a "Village Idiot." Brown County is to idiots as Saudi Arabia is to oil.

"Village Idiot" is an honorific title that bestows upon the recipient bragging rights and a $100 bar tab. The qualifications for this office are simple: one must do something particularly stupid, and must be a customer or employee of the Story Inn. (It is not a requirement for one to be a "natural born idiot".) Though the term of "Idiot" only lasts for one year, an "Idiot" may be elected more than once (it's never happened).

Past nominees include:

- A Story bartender who set her own hair on fire as she was attempting to tame her coiffure with hairspray. (The unfortunate incident did not persuade her to give up smoking.)
- A tavern regular who somehow managed to run over her own foot while driving her own truck.
- A Story employee who, while learning to hunt with a bow and arrow, brought down his own Chevy Cavalier.
- A bar patron (with an engineering degree from Purdue, no less) who filled a kiddie pool on the wood deck behind his house. The weight of the water (8.3 lbs./gallon x 1000) caused the deck to separate from his house and collapse into a heap of twisted lumber.
- A Story regular who decided to propose marriage to his girlfriend at our Valentine's Wine Dinner. He arrived, and realized he'd forgotten the ring. He called the only person who could fetch it for him—his ex-wife—who dutifully brought it to the dinner.
- A Story Inn server who attempted to verify the authenticity of a Story Inn gift certificate by repeatedly calling the Story Inn from the Story Inn's front desk. She could not understand why the other line kept ringing when she called out.
- A wine dinner guest who drank the contents of the dump bucket on a bet from his wife.
- A bar patron who mistakenly took his dog's mange medicine; his wife claims it fixed a weak patch on his beard.

- A Story housekeeper who got her hair caught in a vacuum cleaner and needed to call for help to get it extracted.
- A bar regular who insisted that a human body adds weight to an already full bathtub. The same person also contended that sound travels slower when you're in an airplane.
- A frequent guest who proved herself worthy of her blond hair by embarking on a cross-country road trip, leaving her sandwiches on the roof of the car.
- A musician who hit a cow on his way to perform at the Story Inn. (The cow was unharmed. However, his Honda Civic needed a new side mirror.)
- A 93 year-old woman who crawled under a table and bit a man on the leg in an effort to get his attention.

Jane Ammeson, by the way, earned an "Idiot" nomination when she found herself locked in the Story Inn's General Store at 3 a.m., wearing a tiara.

The bartender at Story accepts ballots for "Village Idiot" beginning in January. In true Chicago fashion, one can vote early, and often.

In 2006, I won the election for "Village Idiot" for a lifetime of achievement. Some specifics: I hit myself on the head with a hammer while attempting to hang a birdhouse. I drove off with my laptop computer on the roof of the car. My ineptitude with power tools is legendary; once I struggled to put a single screw into a block of wood, not realizing that the power drill was set to rotate in the wrong direction. As a fill-in for the bartender, I once asked a customer to describe the ingredients of a rum and coke.

I'm messy, in a way that cannot be easily dismissed as a charming eccentricity. Some time back, my car became so full of trash that a field mouse took up residence in it, feasting on hamburger buns, pizza crust and ice melt (in the cup holder), until I finally cleaned it out.

When playing the game "Trivial Pursuit," I have never gotten a correct answer in the "Popular Culture" category. I am incapable of grasping the genre known as the "Reality Show," and do not care what Ryan Lochte would do under any conceivable set of circumstances. But now I do give the "Realty Show" genre grudging respect as a means to launch a political career.

I am befuddled by Facebook. I do not have a Facebook account, and never will, because I cannot fathom why anyone would want to share trivial facts about their lives with strangers and hand that information over to the NSA in a package wrapped with a bow.

That's especially true when it pertains to private relationships. I am keen to the machinations of Rasputin and Machiavelli, but do not know, or care to know, or speculate as to who, or what, the Kardashians, Miley Cyrus, Madonna, Bill Clinton or Donald Trump might be doing what with.

Chapter 7. The Political "Climate"

> "Cherish those who seek the truth but beware of those who find it."
>
> — Voltaire

Among the issues which divide Reds and Royal Blues at both the local and national level is "climate change" f/k/a "global warming."

A good number of Republicans, and all "Redneck Reds," deny that climate change is happening at all. They accuse Royal Blues of perpetrating an elaborate hoax to bankrupt coal companies, extend the reach of government regulation, and compel us all to drive electric cars. Royal Blues, on the other hand, believe climate change to be the biggest threat to humanity since the election of Ronald Reagan. It is caused, they reason, exclusively by our burning of fossil fuels. Royal Blues view every instance of aberrant weather as confirmation of this conviction.

Both sides are wrong. Unfortunately, for reasons I'll lay out shortly, neither can be proven wrong, at least not within the puny lifetime of anyone making such smug pronouncements today.

From a geologic perspective, there has always been "climate change." Most of Indiana was buried under a glacier as recently as 22,000 years ago. Long before that, most of Indiana was once a shallow tropical sea, which is why we have limestone here in such abundance. The land itself migrated here from the equator, in a process called continental drift. Continents can move about as fast as a human's fingernails can grow, and over eons, continents can travel considerable distances.

Since the earth's crust solidified some 4.5 billion years ago, the sun has gotten hotter. Today, solar output is about 30% higher than it used to be. And it is growing hotter. In another 4.5 billion years or so from now, the earth itself will be engulfed by the sun, and everything here burned to a cinder. We can buy ourselves a billion years or so by migrating to Mars.

Ever since the LGM, glaciers have been in full retreat everywhere on earth. When we witness a glacier receding today, we might plausibly attribute that to a natural cycle that occurs over tens or hundreds of thousands of years. Or, as is currently fashionable among Royal Blues, we could blame it all on the automobile, which came into common use barely a century ago.

At the dawn of the industrial revolution, when humans first began to mine sequestered carbon and burn it for fuel, the earth's atmosphere contained about 280 parts per million of carbon dioxide. Two and a half centuries later, it stands at about 400 ppm. That's a 40% increase in a geologic instant, and this increase can mostly be blamed on the cumulative assault of humanity's smoke stacks and tail-pipes, and penchant for mowing down trees and eating Big Macs.

No one can deny that CO_2 is a greenhouse (i.e., heat-trapping) gas. No one can deny that there's more of it in the air than we had two and a half centuries ago. And no one can deny that humanity is responsible for that increase.

But let's put this into perspective, please.

First of all, as producers of greenhouse gas, we humans are a puny force. Each year, more than five times as much CO_2 is produced by Mother Nature than by humans, on average, and that has been going on for millions of years. The natural burning for forests, or the natural decomposition of forest detritus, or the occasional volcanic eruption, produces prodigious quantities of the stuff, putting us to shame.

So why is the earth not a hellish inferno? Because life on earth has developed an exquisite mechanism for sequestering carbon, called photosynthesis. Plants eat the stuff and bury it in their tissues. Herbivores eat the plants and bury it in their tissues. The ocean's stock of phytoplankton alone scrubs 50 billion tons of carbon out of the atmosphere each year, converting it into organic mass for the ocean's inhabitants to eat. That's as much biochemical fixation as goes on in all the world's continents combined.

The added CO_2 is stimulating plant growth everywhere, both land and sea, just as adding fertilizer to a field improves the growth, and yield, of corn. Kentuckiana's massive young forest is adding hugely to its biomass each year, making it a carbon sink, even with all its people driving SUVs and pick-up trucks with stick families pasted on the back window.

Some of this biomass (in fact, the great majority of it) goes back into the atmosphere, after a short delay, when the plants or animals die and decompose. However, some small percentage of it stays sequestered, dropping into a swamp or into the depths of the ocean, not to return to the air. That's how we got the coal and oil that we burn today. Indiana's limestone is really just solid carbon dioxide, sequestered by carbonate-shelled creatures that died eons ago and became pressed into sedimentary rock. That's our pillar to denote the Ten O'Clock Treaty line at the Story Inn.

Carbon is being scrubbed from the air by chemical processes as well. The ocean, covering about 70% of the earth's surface, scrubs CO_2 from the air ($CO_2 + H_2O = H + HCO_3$). So does rain. The world's oceans and lakes currently hold 50 times as much carbon as the atmosphere. (Unfortunately, capturing carbon in this way alters its pH, disrupting ecosystems.)

Thus, there's already a carbon burial mechanism in place, and it's been in place for a lot longer than there's been an EPA or Royal Blues to pontificate about it. We're just tipping the scale a bit. And scientists have recently recognized that the enriched atmosphere has done much to stimulate photosynthesis and, therefore, the process of carbon fixation. Scientific consensus is that carbon uptake has increased so markedly that it is scrubbing about half of the stuff humans are now adding to the air each year. And this also occurred in a geologic instant, a mere couple of centuries.

Second of all, in terms of earth's geologic history, the level of CO_2 was at an unprecedentedly low level at the dawn of the industrial revolution. In fact, atmospheric CO_2 may have been lower in the mid-18th century than it was at any other time in earth's very, very long history. By sheer coincidence, earth was starved for CO_2 at precisely the time we humans started pulling coal and oil out of the ground and burning it.

Plant life was beginning to adapt to the dearth of CO_2 just as we humans came to the rescue. The so-called C-4s need much less of it to fix sugars, and therefore can thrive in an impoverished atmosphere consisting of only 280 ppm. The less efficient C-3's may well have been on their way to extinction.

Third of all, despite CO_2's undeniable heat-trapping properties, there is only a tenuous link between high CO_2 and warm temperatures through geologic time. Scientists are at a loss to explain why, but facts are facts.

During the Jurassic Period 200 million years ago, earth's atmosphere contained about 1800 ppm of CO_2, about 4.5 times what it is today. During the Cambrian Period 560 million years ago, it was nearly 7000 ppm, about 17 times higher than today. The Cambrian Period is recognized as the time when evolution went into hyper drive. Evolutionary biologists call it the "Cambrian Explosion," for good reason. Obviously, the high CO_2 made the Cambrian ocean more acidic than today's ocean, though not enough to turn a piece of Kentuckiana limestone into an Alka-Seltzer tablet.

The late Ordovician Period was an ice age, and CO_2 concentrations were 4400 ppm, about 11 times what they are today. According to the greenhouse theory, Earth should have been exceedingly hot, but it wasn't. Clearly, other factors besides atmospheric carbon influence earth's temperature.

We are at the dawn of the Anthropocene Epoch, a time when humans have become a geologic force without understanding what it means to be a geologic force. There's more than seven billion of us now. That inevitably leaves a footprint. For example, scientists have found traces of lead, once released from the combustion of leaded gasoline, in mud that has settled at the bottom of the sea. Over geologic time, that will morph into rock, thereby cementing our role as a geologic force.

Climate does change, and it always will change. There is nothing that we humans can do to stop it. We can, and should, assess whether we are having an impact on an already changing world, and if we are, assess what kind of impact that might be. And if it's a bad impact we have, then we should realistically assess what we can do to minimize it.

Here's another dose of *Realpolitik*: since climate changes over geologic time, no Redneck Red or Royal Blue alive today will have the satisfaction of being vindicated. Royal Blues will continue to blame the weather (e.g., Hurricane Sandy, more recent flooding in Louisiana and North Carolina) on climate change, which is myopic, but at least no Redneck Red can prove them wrong.

Politicians, who believe themselves uniquely situated to know what is best for us, are currently seeking approval for an international accord they claim will cap CO_2 emissions at precisely the point it would take to keep the planet from warming more than two degrees Celsius. This is the height of eco-arrogance, in my view.

No scientist alive can tell you the extent to which the added CO_2 is warming the planet, or even if it's the reason its appears to be warming at all (yes, it is warming). And no scientist has yet to fully explain the carbon burial mechanism that has been in place for eons, and which has shifted into high-gear just as we began tipping the scale. But somehow, despite the dearth of evidence, politicians have contrived their own formula that equates a specific rise in CO_2 precisely to a two degree rise in global temperatures, and have declared that to be the tipping point to Armageddon. Only a politician can turn a sundial into an atomic clock.

The stupidity doesn't end there. The politicians then eschew the most efficient method of achieving their stated objective of creating a low-carbon economy: a carbon tax. Throw a tax on gasoline, and people will burn less of it. They will demand more fuel-efficient cars, and drive less. This will have the added benefit of reducing traffic congestion and clearing up smog in urban areas, and providing revenue to fix the roads we have, and maybe to build an occasional public transportation system that isn't dedicated to expressing our gratitude to a Congressman. No, the politicians have decreed that they will meet our low-carbon objectives through administrative regulations, complex tax incentives and subsidies for dubious "green" energy projects, and a ridiculous, contrived "market" trading the very thing we're trying to get rid of.

There are many, many things I do not understand. For example, I cannot understand how a politician could dedicate an entire life to "public service" earning a middling salary, yet retire rich.

For my part, I'm happy to proclaim my ignorance about climate change and defer such discussions away from the realm of politics to the realm of pure science.

The fact of climate change should not divide left and right. Study facts, not politics.

Chapter 8. Corpus Juris Longinqui Ruris

> "I am ashamed the law is such an ass."
> —George Chapman, 1559–1654

Corpus Juris Ruris I: Real Property.

Redneck Reds own most of the private land in Brown County, which means they pay most of the local taxes, too. Bruised Blues, who do most of the breeding in Brown County, benefit from the fact that the schools no longer have dirt floors. In this manner, there is a net transfer of wealth from Reds to Blues. Unfortunately, the local schools suck, so they do little to elevate the prevailing level of intelligence of the public at large.

22. Thanks to Republicans, schools now have plumbing, too.

There is one thing that unites Redneck Reds, Bruised Blues, and Royal Blues in Brown County: They all hate change.

23. People in these parts don't like change.

Change, or the fear of change to be more precise, is a powerful motivating force. And when people in Brown County seek to change the use of their land, the community will unite against them as predictably as the sun will rise in the east. The raw merit of the particular requested land use change, or the benefits that such change will confer upon the community at large, is irrelevant. A decade ago, I had the temerity to seek to have Story re-zoned. In my case, I sought some flexibility to repurpose some buildings at Story. We are, after all, a business. It was good for me, and, I believed, for the community as well: more jobs, higher taxes paid for schools, etc.

You would have thought I intended to build a toxic waste dump.

Benjamin and Cynthia Schultz (that's Benjamin, and Cynthia Schultz—Benjamin has no last name) had the place zoned "Planned Unit Development," or "PUD" in the 1980s. Under the PUD, every building had precisely one authorized use. For example, the PUD had designated the barn to be a "picnic shelter." Among other things, I wanted to use the barn to host weddings. This was impermissible under the PUD, and required a zoning change.

In Brown County, as in other places where tribal culture prevails (Afghanistan, Scotland, Myanmar, Washington DC), rumor is far more intriguing than fact. Rumor trumps the truth the moment it is uttered, and once it has repeated often enough, it morphs into a tautology. Hitler called this the "Big Lie," and used it to great effectiveness. Contemporary politicians like Donald Trump seem to have caught on as well.

At the zoning hearing, I was confronted by an officious Royal Blue named Michael Mullett, who had persuaded a posse of locals that I intended to turn Story into another Nashville, replete with over 200 stores each serving caramel corn. This was not my intention at all, but there was no practical way to persuade my neighbors otherwise. No one, including Michael Mullett, bothered to pick up the phone to ask my intentions before organizing the posse.

By this time, the locals had decided that I was a human, and not really from Mars. However, given my ethnic-sounding surname, rumor quickly surfaced that I was Jewish, not really German. Never in my life have I been the recipient of so much undeserved praise.

That zoning experience was my introduction to a peculiar form of property ownership, one which I had not studied in law school, and one which I struggle to fully grasp today. I believe it to be unique to Kentuckiana. But there are a great many things about the law outside of Kentuckiana that I do not understand. For example, why the federal government requires manufacturers to label bottled drinking water as fat free and warn consumers that a package of peanuts might contain nuts.

Under the British Common Law, the private ownership of real property is a protected legal right. A man's home is his castle, so to speak. That notion is very much alive in Common Law countries today, as well as in any country which is economically developed. One can "own" land, and ownership generally means that you can do what you want with it.

In Brown County, real property is not owned by individuals. It is owned communally. And the strength of one's claim to communal property ownership is a function of only two things: (a) the distance your residence is from the property on which you are staking your communal claim; and (b) the length of time that has passed since your kinfolk moved into the County. The shorter the former, and the longer the latter, the stronger your communal property claim. This, in turn, confers upon you the authority to dictate to your neighbor how he or she may use his or her property.

True, we have a recorder's office in Brown County, and one may search the records and find the "owner" of any parcel of property in question. And it is the exclusive burden of such "owner" to pay taxes on it. But that is where the concept of private property ownership in Brown County ends, and the notion of communal property ownership takes over.

At our zoning hearing years ago numerous remonstrators of all political stripes appeared and exercised their oratorical skills. Without exception, they would begin thusly: "I'm so and so, and I live at such and such, which is about so and so miles from Story, and my family has been in this County for EIGHTY YEARS" (emphasis on the "eighty years"). This opening statement established the strength of their respective claims to communal land ownership.

The stronger the claim, the more credible their opposition to my wanting to turn the barn from a picnic shelter into a wedding venue. The local Plan Commission, which enforces such claims to communal property, would listen intently and weigh these statements accordingly. No one seemed to question the premise that one could acquire an interest in real property just by living nearby for a very long time. Under the Common Law, property rights, such as easements appurtenant or restrictive covenants, "run with the land," meaning they attach to the real estate and not to the benefit of a particular person or persons. Not so in Brown County, where property rights "run with the clan."

Now, I will be the first person to accept the premise that ownership of a historic property carries with it certain ethical responsibilities to future generations. It is my fervent desire that Story continue in existence, its architectural and historical integrity intact, long after my remains have turned to dust to enrich the soil of some yet unborn person's vegetable garden. But none of my neighbors seemed interested in preserving either history or architecture. They just didn't want me to use the barn for weddings, even if it meant a job for cousin Billy-Bob and textbooks for the local schoolkids.

We ultimately won the zoning war, and contrary to the dire predictions of Michael Mullett, the earth did not fall off its axis, and Story did not turn into a megalopolis. But the screams of angry remonstrators resonate with me today. It was an unusually bitter struggle, because Mullett was a lawyer with a lot of time on his hands and had a wife who had owned property adjacent to Story for a very long time.

As Tip O'Neill said, all politics is local. Some people call it "NIMBY-ism." We see it on a national level, with former Senator Harry Reid successfully remonstrating against the safe disposal of spent nuclear fuel at Yucca Mountain in his home state. Instead, we deposit it into drums and allow it to molder in populated areas like New Jersey.

There's also a local twist on a legal concept pertaining to the acquisition of real property, adverse possession. This is a well-established notion under the Common Law. In most states, one can legally acquire title to real property by occupying it in an open, notorious, exclusive manner for more than 20 consecutive years. But by law, one cannot take government land by adverse possession. Brown County, and possibly greater Kentuckiana, is the exception.

Several folks who have property backing up to either the Brown County State Park or the Hoosier National Forest have staked claims well into those government lands and will defend their claims with firearms. I have been run off public lands by angry locals for "trespassing." One does not argue with a Hillbilly carrying a gun, so under such circumstances, it is advisable to beat a strategic retreat and live to hike another day.

Corpus Juris Ruris II: Personal Property and Bailments.

Brown County natives have peculiar rules on bailments and title to personal property as well. Personal property is, of course, tangible property that is not affixed to real estate. In Brown County, the most valuable personal property that one can own and possess typically is a pick-up truck, the contents of a tool box and, of course, firearms. But it can include a lot of other things, like scaffolding, a chain saw, sump pump, jumper cables or a pressure washer.

In Brown County, it is a neighborly thing to allow someone to "borrow" your truck or tools. But unlike other places, it is not incumbent upon the borrower to bring it back. You must ask for it back. And if you fail to ask for it back within a reasonable period of time, you could easily lose title to it. In Brown County, it is presumed that you have abandoned your personal property by not asking for it back.

The richer you are, or are perceived to be, the quicker that presumption comes into play. Some years ago, we had two employees (husband and wife) whose car ceased to function. They asked to "borrow" the pick-up truck that we keep here on property for odd jobs. I assented, with the thought that they'd be on their feet in a day or two and would have the means of transporting themselves to work in the meantime.

The truck quickly became "their" vehicle. A couple of weeks later, hearing nothing and watching the recyclables pile up, I asked for them to return it. The outrage was palpable, and they both quit their jobs in righteous indignation. (For reasons which elude me, I've always been perceived to be rich, so it was a *faux pas* for me not to ask for it back sooner.)

Likewise, it is fine to "borrow" something in Brown County, even without the owner's consent, so long as you intend to bring it back or replace it. Employees routinely "borrow" carpet cleaners, vacuums, nail guns, etc., and in the vast majority of cases do bring them back. It is unnerving, being unfamiliar with such concepts, to fruitlessly search for an item only to find that someone had "borrowed" it. (Locals say "barr-eed".)

Mercifully, in cases where someone has "borrowed" something without the owner's knowledge or consent, there is no presumption of abandonment when the owner fails to ask for it back. This is an equitable exception to Brown County's law of bailments, it being recognized that one cannot demand the return of something that you don't know is missing, or in whose possession it might be.

Some years back, only minutes after I had spoken to an employee, I saw him draining our lawn mower gas into his car. I was peeved, because the nearest gas station is 10 miles away, and I have little time to fetch a can of gas. He explained that he was only "borrowing" the gas, and that he would replace it. I still wonder why he didn't ask me first before taking it.

Accusing someone of thievery, and not of "borrowing," is tantamount to slander and is an insult not only to the "borrower" but to his or her entire family as well. Those grudges can last for generations.

Some years ago, I caught an employee "borrowing" my son's jeep, which he had to hot-wire to get to run. My son happened to be in Europe at the time, presumably with the keys in his pocket. The "borrower's" explanation: "I needed it to get home. Besides, I put gas in it."

I couldn't argue with that logic.

Corpus Juris Ruris III: Master and Servant/Employment Discrimination

Brown County has its own employment law as well, and these new concepts governing the employer-employee relationship have gained acceptance in other parts of Kentuckiana, too.

The British Common Law we inherited in this country gave us the "employment at will" doctrine. An employer could fire an employee for any reason, at any time. This doctrine has slowly changed. Although the "at will" doctrine survives in name, the employment relationship has in fact morphed into a property right as well.

Thus, an employer can sometimes now be sued for "wrongful discharge," a concept that is irreconcilable to the precept that employees serve their masters "at will." The primary exceptions to the "at will" doctrine began with sensible legislative changes, prohibiting employers from firing people for certain reasons unrelated to job performance (e.g., simply for being black).

In Brown County, the employment relationship has developed even further. Being hired creates entitlements which were never contemplated either under the Common Law or subsequent state or federal legislation.

One of those is the right to receive unemployment compensation even after quitting a job or being sacked from your job for good cause.

The law outside of Kentuckiana, of course, recognizes that one may not claim unemployment benefits after being fired "for cause." But in Brown County and other parts of Kentuckiana, "for cause" is interpreted very narrowly. Likewise, quitting a job may be entirely justified under the right set of circumstances, entitling one to unemployment benefits.

In Kentuckiana, "My car won't start" will serve to justify a limitless number of late-shows or no-shows. Any employer who would presume to hold an employee accountable for his own transportation to work is acting wrongfully, triggering eligibility for unemployment benefits. (Amazingly, Kentuckianans never seem to be afflicted with car troubles on payday.)

We've had kitchen employees file for unemployment compensation after being canned for "borrowing" a beef tenderloin. We've had employees who simply failed to show up for work after five or so shifts, and then filed for unemployment. One had the audacity to file for unemployment while she still was working here. The Notice of Unemployment Claim arrived in the mail during her shift. We had no plans to lay her off, but as I learned later, she had plans to leave, and simply acted pre-emptively to get her benefits.

For the working poor in Brown County/Kentuckiana, employment is often not a path to a career but a measure of how long one must endure work, or the semblance of work, until one becomes eligible for the public dole. Coastal elites, even people as lucid as JD Vance, erroneously refer to these people as "working class." I see no point in labeling people by the very thing they're trying to avoid.

Uniformly, employees are indignant when they face opposition to a claim for benefits. Very few grasp the concept that this is not a free lunch: the employer ultimately pays, in the form of a higher unemployment insurance rating. Small businesses cannot print money. Only the federal government can do that.

Periodically, a bureaucrat or a politician somewhere decrees that we must raise the minimum wage, or raise threshold management compensation to qualify for the wage/hour exemption under the Fair Labor Standards Act. Such edicts, though well-intentioned, are damaging to small Kentuckiana businesses in the extreme. They are based on two false assumptions: (a) that the cost of living is same everywhere, and (b) that people make a career of working at a dish tank.

In point of fact, money stretches a lot further in Kentuckiana than it does in New York or California, and the minimum wage is paid only for entry-level jobs, ideally as a pathway to something much better. In practice, we pay a lot more than minimum wage for most jobs, because the employees have earned it. A high school kid getting his/her first job here needs to start low, and then prove to us that he/she is worth more than that.

I am quite aware that some of our best long-term employees sometimes make ends meet with food stamps and/or the Earned Income Tax Credit, and that all of them drive on roads that are, to greater or lesser degrees, paved. Coastal elites see that as a subsidy to this business, and not to the people who are working and struggling to make ends meet. They overlook the critical fact that all such employees are much better off with the job they have than with no job at all.

Every responsible small business owner pays his/her employees, as well as taxes and vendors, before reaping any benefits at all. They do this while working under the boot of clueless bureaucrats who receive a reliable paycheck, health insurance, a government-funded pension, and get to take Dr. Martin Luther King's birthday off with full pay. It was tough to hear our own president proclaim recently: "You didn't build that."

In this bastion of free enterprise that is America, the proprietors of small businesses are held strictly liable for knowing the difference between an "employee" and a "subcontractor," even though the law itself is not clear on this point. And if the small business has "employees" and not "subcontractors" working for it, then that small business has the further burden of serving as the government's unpaid collector of such employees' taxes, judgments and child support obligations. If an employer fails in this mandate, he or she may face fines, or even jail time.

Thus, when the Child Support Division finally catches up with a deadbeat dad and serves us with a garnishment order, we have no choice but to comply.

This situation is actually much worse for employers inside Brown County/Kentuckiana than it is for employers on the outside, due to the peculiarities of the employer-employee relationship that prevails here. When an employees' paycheck first arrives showing a child support deduction, it predictably elicits a squeal, which is always followed by this conversation:

(Employee's knock on the door)

Manager: "Hi Hunter. What can I do for you?"

Employee (holding a pay stub): "Uh, you took too much out of my check."

Manager: "Well, Hunter, let's look at the withholding order. (Papers rustling.) Ah, here it is. No Hunter, I'm sorry, but that's the correct withholding amount. See, it says here that you owe five years of arrearages too."

Employee: "It ain't right. She won't let me see Hunter, Jr., and I'm not paying."

Manager: "I'm really sorry, but our hands are tied."

Employee (incredulously): "The system ain't fair. I shouldn't pay if I can't see my kid. Why didn't you stop them?"

Manager: "Because we can't."

Employee (getting angry): "Well, I can't live off of this. I need a raise."

Manager: "Hunter, you've only been here six weeks. Your first review will happen in four months."

Employee (getting angrier): "This ain't fair!"

Manager (calming voice): "Could you cut back on something? Maybe give up cigarettes?"

Employee: "(Expletive deleted) I quit."

This conversation is inevitably followed by the filing of an unemployment claim.

Here's the employee's reasoning under established Brown County/ Kentuckiana law: It is the employer's, not the employee's, burden to challenge the fairness of withholding orders, and the failure to do so is a breach of the fiduciary duty that the employer owes to the employee in Kentuckiana. This, when coupled with the employer's unreasonable refusal to pay a living wage that includes a basic necessity such as cigarette consumption, constitutes a constructive dismissal without good cause. And this, in turn, triggers the right to receive unemployment compensation.

Racial discrimination is illegal everywhere. But more important than that, bigotry is bad for business. Despite Kentuckiana's curse of being overwhelmingly white and Christian, employment discrimination is actually quite rare. That does not mean that Kentuckiana businesses do not feel the boot of the EEOC and other agencies on their necks.

The proprietors of small businesses in America are held strictly liable for knowing the race of their employees, even though the federal government fails to define "race" with any degree of clarity, and makes it illegal to ask your employees to identify their "race" either before or after you hire them. I'm not making this up.

At the Story Inn, we attempt to hire the most competent people for the job. Race is irrelevant. We're not allowed to ask the "race" of our applicants, but we wouldn't do that anyway. There is no correlation between race and competence.

But the US Census Bureau periodically sends us a questionnaire which requires us to identify the "race" of each employee and to sign that document under penalties of perjury. If we fail to file the form, we face a fine and possible jail time. If the Census Bureau thinks we're lying on that form, we face a fine, and possible jail time. If we can't answer the questionnaire because we don't know, and ask the employee to help us, we face a fine, civil damages, and, of course, public excoriation at the hands of Progressive "journalists" everywhere.

Here's an 18th century liberal's definition of "race":

If you walk on two feet and brush your teeth, you are human. If you are human, you came from Africa. We humans have settled all over the world, at different times, beginning a mere few tens of thousands of years ago. That's not enough time for evolution driven by natural selection to fundamentally change who we are.

Melanin is a pigment of skin that protects it from the tropical sun and helps prevent cancer. We all started off with dark skin when we lived in Africa. But in temperate regions, people became strongly selected for lighter-colored skin due to the lack of vitamin D, which was causing birth defects. Those people lost some of that melanin. Some light-skinned people who left Africa have since returned to Africa. We have always mixed, and we will continue to mix. We can produce fertile offspring with anyone we come into contact with. Human skin is now a mélange of colors, all of them skin-deep.

Therefore, "race" is an artificial construct with no meaning. Get over it.

Here's how the Census Bureau defines "race" for small business owners:

"The US Census Bureau must adhere to the 1997 Office of Management and Budget (OMB) standards of race and ethnicity which guide the Census Bureau in classifying written responses to the race question:

• White—A person having origins in any of the original peoples of Europe, the Middle East, or North Africa.

• Black or African American—a person having origins in any of the Black racial groups of Africa.

• American Indian or Alaska Native—A person having origins in any of the original peoples of North and South America (including Central America) and who maintains a tribal affiliation or community attachment.

• Asian—A person having origins in any of the original peoples of the Far East, Southeast Asia, or the Indian subcontinent including, for example, Cambodia, China, India, Japan, Korea, Malaysia, Pakistan, the Philippine Islands, Thailand and Vietnam.

• Native Hawaiian or Other Pacific Islander—A person having origins in any of the original peoples of Hawaii, Guam, Samoa, or other Pacific Islands."

Source: census.gov/topics/population/race/about.html

So, what do the words "origin" and "original people" mean, if we all came from the same place? Those arriving in a specific location 100 years ago?

1,000? 10,000? I don't recall any of these countries existing when humans originally settled there.

Until just a couple of thousand years ago, everyone lived a nomadic life, so which wandering clan is the Census Bureau referring to? The first to arrive and settle down in a specific place? The second? The tenth? What about people who haven't settled down yet? What about people who came, and then moved on? What of people of mixed ancestry? Does it matter when or where they mixed?

"American Indians" and "Alaskan Natives" all migrated here from Asia, when an ice age conveniently opened up a land bridge. They didn't mix with anyone else, until Europeans arrived with their black slaves. Why are these people not "Asians"?

The Chinese think that "Han" is a race. Who are we to lump them together with Koreans and Japanese?

When I read stuff this imbecilic, it literally makes me want to cry.

I once called the Census Bureau to seek counsel in dealing with this conundrum, and a lady soothingly recommended that I give my "best educated guess." I don't know about you, but I have a problem making an "educated guess" about something that I can't define, am forbidden to inquire about, and don't think exists in the first place, and then swear under penalties of perjury that it is accurate in order to avoid incarceration at the whim of a bureaucrat.

Our government is determined to divide us and bestow benefits upon some citizens to the exclusion of others. Such is the mandate from coastal Progressives and do-gooders in Washington. They're trying to atone for some dreadful things that light-skinned people did to darker-skinned people a long time ago, long before any of us were born.

As a lawyer, I once faced the challenge of assisting a client attempting to qualify before the Small Business Administration as a "Section 8(a) minority-owned small business enterprise." (American bureaucrats have a fetish for acronyms, so this was conventionally known as an "SBA-MBE".) Our federal government sets aside contracts for "qualified MBEs," meaning they do not have to endure the inconvenience of bidding competitively for government contracts.

As with every government goodie, it was necessary to fill out a complex form to get it, which included the applicant's description of what it has been like to endure the slings and arrows of racial discrimination. I gave it my best shot, describing what it was like to grow up as a poor black child on the mean streets of Indianapolis.

It worked. The client became a qualified MBE, and that's when I realized that I might have a talent for writing fiction. I'm not making this up.

Ours is not the first government in history to classify people by "race" and treat them differently. The best example of a recent attempt to do so occurred in apartheid South Africa, where the government did its best to segregate people into "homelands" and "suburbs" based upon whether they were "white," "black," "colored" (i.e., mixed race) or "Indian." The South Africans then couldn't define race any better than our own government can do today, so they passed a "Population Registration Act" and issued ID cards to its citizens. To catch the inevitable cheaters in the registration process, the apartheid regime concocted a simple test that actually had a veneer of objectivity to it: if you were dark-skinned and could run a comb through your hair, you were "colored"; otherwise, you were "black." To give credit where it is due, the South Africans, at least, didn't place the burden of classifying its people upon its private employers.

It would come as a relief among small business owners in America today if the Census Bureau would learn a lesson from their apartheid kin and simply issue combs, and allow us to objectively report the degree of resistance as we passed it through employees' coiffures. Unfortunately, the Census Bureau's classification categories differ from those four under apartheid (a comb will pass as easily through an Asian's hair as a white person's hair), so employing government-issued combs would have little practical use. Technology has improved recently, so maybe the Census Bureau could furnish a spectrometer to detect the prevalence of melanin. We'd have to administer the test before Spring Break, when "white" people run off to warmer climes for a dose of vitamin D.

All of this, of course, goes well beyond the Constitution's mandate to conduct a census so that we could apportion seats in the US House of Representatives every ten years. The last I checked, people of color could vote, and being employed is not a condition of suffrage.

In Kentuckiana, small businesses run a dreadful risk of hiring only "white" people, because the population here is almost all "white." Fortunately, our workforce at the Story Inn has more melanin, on average, than does the Kentuckiana population at large, so we're probably OK if a federal bureaucrat rolls into town looking to instigate a race riot.

Corpus Juris Ruris IV: Disability.

By far, the most coveted employee entitlement of all is "disability." Regrettably, since about 2009, the federal government has been handing out Social Security disability benefits to able-bodied people in an apparent effort to soak up long-term unemployment. To someone outside of Brown County/Kentuckiana, a *bona fide* disability (i.e., a condition which prevents one from being gainfully employed) is a tragic circumstance which would merit sending a Hallmark sympathy card. To someone inside Brown County/ Kentuckiana, a disability is an achievement which would merit sending a Hallmark congratulatory card.

"Disability" means that one need no longer pursue the charade of being employed, or seeking employment, and expect to receive a monthly stipend sufficient to cover the cost of food, cigarettes and the satellite bill, in perpetuity. Life doesn't get any better than that, especially if you can score a prescription for OxyContin too.

In Brown County, disability is a game changer. Some years back, we had a dishwasher excitedly inform me that he "might get disability." By all appearances, he was able-bodied and had never once informed us that he suffered from any sort of physical or mental impairment. He quit his job, without notice, the moment he became eligible for his check. Simultaneously, he bought a new truck.

I, of course, had to hire someone to replace him, so the unemployment rate did, in fact, go down. Score one for the politicians.

Once you're on "disability," it doesn't mean that you must sacrifice a single creature comfort. If you need cash for a Bud Light, or even a trip to the Gulf coast of Alabama for a holiday at the "Redneck Riviera," you can always work under the table. There's always pocket change to be earned from cutting grass, chopping wood, scrapping metal, growing pot, "borrowing" stuff, or cooking meth. By legalizing marijuana, we could eliminate a lot of poverty in America's flyover middle, in my modest opinion.

No matter how hard the government tries, it will never stamp out the underground economy in America's flyover middle. The government is, however, doing a splendid job of exterminating legitimate, tax-paying small businesses here.

CHAPTER 9. THE CONSTITUTION AND THE FLYOVERS

> "I would not look to the U.S. Constitution
> if I were drafting a constitution (today)."
>
> —Justice Ruth Bader Ginsburg

Everyone seems to have an opinion about the Constitution, especially those who have not bothered to read it, having acquired their understanding of it solely by listening to right-wing talk radio.

One of those right-wing radio jocks is Greg Garrison, once a frequent customer of the Inn. Greg usually arrived with some nefarious characters in tow.

Greg and I are both sons of medical doctors who grew up in all-white suburbs, hung out at segregated country clubs, attended IU, then law school, sired white children, and then went on to careers in the legal profession. As a lawyer, Greg received kudos when he successfully prosecuted Mike Tyson for raping a young woman in an Indianapolis hotel room in 1991. I never received such public adoration for filing a Hart-Scott-Rodino Form with the Justice Department, an act that enabled an Indianapolis company named Conseco to go public, and a whole lot of innocent people to lose their savings. (My partner in that endeavor, Larry Inlow from Harvard Law School, literally lost his head over that matter when a helicopter blade ended his reign as America's most highly compensated lawyer.)

Despite these seemingly parallel lives, Greg and I bear few similarities, particularly with respect to our sartorial style and political *Weltanschauung*. I wear khaki shorts and Birkenstocks. Greg wears cowboy boots, vest and hat, and, in true cowboy fashion, carries a loaded Smith & Wesson and a razor-sharp pocket knife. Greg has a peculiar cowboy affectation, in speech as well as demeanor, which I might infer he did not acquire by spending his formative years in the suburbs of Indianapolis. Maybe he studied for the Indiana Bar Exam in Wyoming while he was working for a cattle rancher.

As an 18th Century liberal, my harshest criticism of Greg can only be this: he salts his food before he tastes it, and he's a lousy tipper.

After I was beat up by that meth-head in front of the Inn, Greg persuaded me to buy a .38 and get a concealed carry permit. They're easy to come by in flyover America. A .38 would be an excellent equalizer were I to be confronted by Mike Tyson, or another meth-head. Greg and I agree that responsible people should be allowed to possess a gun, and that using one should be a very last resort. We do not see eye-to-eye on much else, mostly because Greg's brain has turned to oatmeal. He suffers from a condition known as "Conservative Radio Addiction Progression," or "CRAP."

Greg and other conservatives like the Second Amendment so much that they often stop reading the Constitution right there.

With the notable exception of Switzerland, gun ownership is unusual in Western societies. We now have about as many guns as people in the United States. Yes, we are a boorish society and use them a lot. But given the fact that almost anyone already has, or can easily get, a firearm, it is amazing to me that gun violence is not even more prevalent. If one would bother to compare the prevalence of firearms in specific American cities and the incidences of gun violence (excluding suicide), you would actually find little or no correlation between them.

My German clients were amazed to find out that it was totally legal to walk around Kentuckiana with a firearm—but not an open beer. When such a client visits, I do not attempt to impress them with *Rheinheitsgebot* lager. I take them to a shooting range.

Progressives like Jane Ammeson like the Commerce Clause because they think it created a mandate for the federal government to spawn administrative agencies with unchecked powers, to rectify all of society's wrongs. Progressives dislike the First Amendment's protection of free speech, particularly when someone attempts to exercise that right on a college campus or commits a heinous act of micro-aggression against one of America's anointed class of victims. Jane thinks "hate speech" should be defined as anything that offends the thinnest-skinned American, and should be criminalized.

There were only 4543 words in the original, un-amended version. By comparison, the US Tax Code has over 1,000,000 words, which makes it impenetrable to anyone, including Albert Einstein, who said, "The hardest thing in the world to understand is the income tax." Einstein could describe the merger of space and time but could not grasp the nuances of "C" and "D" corporate mergers, as well as a whole lot of things he appropriately attributed to "black holes." Even Einstein would be taxed to fathom the magnitude of our national debt, which has grown to $20,000,000,000,000.

That's why the Internal Revenue Service has had to issue an additional 4,000,000 words of regulations to clarify these things for us. We have Congress, and bureaucrats, to thank for the lifting of that fog. And we have Keynesians to assure us that our mounting national debt is nothing to worry about, either. (As Alfred E. Newman would say, "What, me worry"?)

Our tax code, and accompanying regulations to clarify it, being too complex for even Einstein to comprehend, inevitably leads to implementation and enforcement that is arbitrary and capricious. It is impossible to know this law; yet, we are held accountable to it by unelected, unchecked bureaucrats. If the IRS auditor happens to hate you, your life can be lost in a tangled legal web. This raises some obvious equal protection issues under the Constitution.

If you choose to fight the auditor, you can take your claim to tax court, where you will face a judge employed by the IRS. And this raises some obvious due process issues/separation of powers questions under the Constitution.

The Roman emperor Caligula is not fondly remembered by history for doing much the same thing. He would allegedly "publish" the laws of Rome on the top of a tall column, in letters so small that citizens could not see it, then enforce those laws with a bloody vengeance. Every now and then, a journalist in this country commits a random act of journalism and writes a compelling account about the IRS targeting a particular political group. I find these stories to be deeply disconcerting, since they chill the expression of free speech guaranteed by the First Amendment of the Constitution. Nobody wants an audit any more than they want cancer.

There's something in the Constitution for everyone, and there's much room for interpretation. That's why appointments to the Supreme Court are so important; there are only nine Justices, and their say is final. Lefties were euphoric at the moment NPR announced the unexpected death of Justice Anton Scalia, but the cheering stopped abruptly on November 8, 2016. Since several of the remaining Justices are sclerotic, the Trump Administration will now have an outsized influence in stocking the Court and therefore in influencing the interpretation of this terse document.

Despite the endless commentary from talking head morons on the right and the left, the US Constitution is a product of real genius. Indeed, the Framers of the Constitution, who gathered in Philadelphia during the sultry summer of 1787, were each smarter, by orders of magnitude, than anyone in Congress today. But the Constitution's real genius, I believe, is derived from the thinkers of the European Enlightenment (Locke and Rousseau in particular). The notion that people possess the power of reason, and even the wisdom, to govern themselves, was a truly radical concept. Career politicians and bureaucrats cannot wrap their brains around that idea today.

The Framers agreed that the Articles of Confederation had failed to create a unified country out of the original 13 English colonies, and so they set out to define the powers of a new federal government. Some things, like providing for the common defense, and the minting of currency, would be exclusively federal. So would be the regulation of interstate commerce, a concept which perhaps was undeservedly given wide berth by the Supreme Court in the years that followed.

Those federal powers would be further divided into three branches: executive, legislative and judicial, and kept accountable to each other and to the population at large. Power corrupts, and the people wielding it had to be kept in check. No one then wanted another King George (any more than we want another George W. today).

When someone bemoans the "gridlock" in Washington, I cannot help but think that gridlock is not such a bad thing at all. Bad things happen when politicians get along. Politicians certainly know what is best for themselves, but they uniformly do not know, or care to know, or care, what is best for their minions.

But the Framers were not in agreement as to what to do about the fact that some states were bigger, and therefore wanted to wield more power, than others. Virginia was many times more populous than New Hampshire. Their solution was a brilliant one: a bicameral legislative branch, with one house having equal representation, and the other proportional to population.

This, of course, required that we have a periodic census. So, how do we count black people?

The framers were most certainly not in agreement with what was to become of the institution of slavery. Some of the Framers were abolitionists, some were themselves slaveholders. And the southern slaveholding states were in no mood to yield this power to any document. Moreover, the slave states wanted to count their slave populations for the purpose of apportioning the House of Representatives, even while denying them the right to vote. Thus was born the "three-fifths compromise," kicking the can down the road for another day, ultimately to be settled at a courthouse at Appomattox about eight decades later, following the bloodiest war in American history.

The actual convention proceedings were held in secret, the windows shuttered to prevent eavesdropping. In the days before air conditioning, when lice were ubiquitous, it must have been insufferable. As night fell, the taverns of Philadelphia would inevitably fill up, and I imagine the real work of negotiation would begin. What I would give to be transported back in time, to be a fly on the wall in Philadelphia in the summer of 1787.

By defining the powers of the federal government, the Framers were also limiting them, or so they thought. Except for those enumerated powers conferred to the federal government under the Constitution, the states would retain their sovereignty. That satisfied the "Federalists" but not the "Anti-Federalists." The latter wanted to have basic human rights spelled out too, rights which the federal government had no power to take away. Thus was born the first ten amendments to the Constitution, better known as the "Bill of Rights." No one today would accuse the Anti-Federalists of gilding the lily.

Our central government has grown, it would be safe to say, well beyond the wildest expectations of the Framers of the Constitution. Some of this growth was the result of the need for uniform rules and regulations governing a society that has become far more complex than the Framers could have foreseen. Some if that growth was necessitated by the fact that our population has mushroomed from five million to 325 million people since then. But unfortunately, much recent growth in government has also been fueled by greed, fear and ignorance.

Greed, because the government hands out benefits like candy, always with strings attached—more control. Once the government acquires power, it does not yield it. Fear, because citizens reflexively burrow into the bosom of government at the first sign of trouble. Ignorance, because too many people labor under the illusion that government solves problems, instead of creating them.

The Bill of Rights may well be our last, best bulwark against even greater government growth and intrusion. Given the leviathan we've birthed in Washington, it makes more sense than ever to enumerate the things the government can't take away from us, rather than to proclaim: "These are your powers, that's all you have, now leave us alone!" Kudos to the Anti-Federalists.

Among those rights spelled-out is the 4th Amendment protection against unreasonable searches and seizures. Sadly, I have witnessed the 4th Amendment's evisceration in my more than three decades of law practice.

Consider Section 702 of the Foreign Intelligence Surveillance Act (FISA), a sweeping federal law which authorizes the NSA, FBI and other branches of the federal government to collect personal, private information from people, either directly or through "partners," without their knowledge or consent. It was a tool which Congress, in the aftermath of the September 11 attacks, deemed necessary to combat terrorism. It was supposed to be a temporary measure when it was enacted, but Congress, in a scarily bipartisan way, has quietly extended it multiple times since then, and has showed no inclination to allow its "sunset" provision to kick in.

Prior to collecting such information, the government agency must obtain an order from a special FISA Court, a new court created under FISA ostensibly to protect Americans from government abuse of basic constitutional rights.

Once in possession of a FISA Order, the governmental agency may demand that its "partners" (such as Verizon, AT&T, Yahoo, Sprint, Google and Facebook), hand over their customers' private data without informing those customers, even if it breaches the terms of an existing privacy policy with those customers. Moreover, FISA provides that such "partners" be immunized for any private claim of damages from customers whose data has been so compromised, and compensated, with government funds, for their effort in complying with the FISA Court Order.

Yes, FISA effectively nullifies the privacy portion of the contract you have with your Internet and mobile phone service providers, and sends you the bill for doing so. Surprise!

This is not to imply that American companies have been uncooperative with government spooks in the past. AT&T, in particular, seems to have been eagerly handing over our personal information to the Feds for a very long time. The AT&T "Long Lines" Building at 33 Thomas Street in Manhattan is putatively a telephone facility, but, as it turns out, is also one of the NSA's most valuable assets. I'm beginning to understand why AT&T always gets federal regulatory approval for its many corporate acquisitions. AT&T's status as a rent-seeking oligopoly hasn't changed much since we knew her as "Ma Bell" and broke her up into "Baby Bells" several decades ago.

The FISA Court meets in secret, only hears the government's side of the story, and, in contravention of centuries of Common Law, never publishes its opinions. Moreover, it almost never declines a government request to capture and mine data. For example, in 2012, the government made 1,856 applications for electronic surveillance. The FISA Court granted every last one of them.

Given such latitude by an obliging Congress, the NSA has since taken to collecting metadata from perfectly law-abiding Americans: our telephone calls, our texts, our locations, our e-mails, our web surfing habits, our credit card purchases, even how fast we're driving. If you're driving late-model car, Big Brother even knows if you're wearing your seat belt. Visualize a blue whale scooping up krill.

Our former Director of National Intelligence, James Clapper, lied to Congress under oath about government surveillance, as it turned out, with impunity; yet Congress seeks the prosecution of Edward Snowden for telling the truth about it. Clapper retired recently, with a vested federal pension worth well over $1 million, while Snowden continues to survive on Ramen noodles while he lives on the lam in that comparative bastion of personal freedom, Russia. Clapper's successor, former Indiana Senator Dan Coats, was sanguine about Clapper's fibbing under oath, and once lobbied Congress on behalf of Sprint to insulate telecommunications companies from liability for spilling its customers' secrets to the government.

It's hard to take the Alfred E. Newman approach to government intrusion of this magnitude.

In spite of such corrosive attacks upon our liberties, the Constitution has served us well. We have enjoyed growth, freedoms and prosperity unprecedented in human history. It's been a good run, but now it's time we amend that document, for reasons that could not have been foreseen by the Framers.

First, the Framers could not have contemplated the ease by which the country could count presidential ballots over thousands of miles and numerous time zones. The Electoral College seemed like a good idea at the time, but technology, and the Internet in particular, has rendered it obsolete. In practice, only a handful of states have contested presidential elections, and only in those states does a vote for president really count. People living in small states, or states which are either solidly Democrat or Republican, are effectively disenfranchised. Twice in the past 16 years—in 2000 and 2016—we have elected a President who did not win the popular vote, let alone a majority of those eligible to vote.

Predictably, a free market in vote-trading has emerged, enabling people in swing states to trade their votes with people in solidly "red" or "blue" states, a practice euphemistically known as "strategic voting." With so much at stake, it's only a matter of time before votes in places like Florida will be auctioned off, legally or otherwise.

The Constitution needs to be changed. One person, one vote, for president, no matter where you happen to live. For reasons I cannot articulate, I recently tuned into Greg Garrison's radio show, where I heard him gloating about Trump's victory and thanking "God" for the Founders' "wisdom" in giving us the Electoral College. That's "CRAP." The right-wing blogosphere is currently alive with praise for the Electoral College because Trump would not have won without it. Bloggers note with satisfaction that Trump "won" some 3,085 counties or parishes to Clinton's 57, which is irrelevant, because in most of those counties or parishes raccoons outnumber people. People vote, raccoons do not.

Ditto, there should be one or more national primary elections to select party candidates for president (more than one primary election may be necessary to narrow the field until a clear majority favorite candidate appears). Too much clout is bestowed upon fringe voters in Iowa and New Hampshire. Direct elections. That's the way it should be, and the Framers, could they be here today, would hardly disagree. They would be aghast at the major parties' choices of candidates for president in recent years.

Second, the Framers could not have contemplated the advances in technology which have enabled the FBI and the NSA to employ laptops, servers, cell phones and even the family car to peer deep into people's anal cavities without their knowledge or consent, or the probable cause to do so. The Bill of Rights clearly contemplates the right of privacy, but nowhere is it specifically spelled out, because there were no such things as laptops, servers or cell phones in 1787. That needs to change.

Third, the Framers could not have contemplated the political culture the federal government has spawned. We fought a war to oust England and its overbearing king. Today, we have an entitled political elite with all the trappings of a monarchy, with special interests (lobbyists) paying tribute. Congress routinely exempts itself from the laws it writes for the rest of us, and engages in behavior (like insider trading, or raiding someone else's trust fund) that would land the rest of us in jail. We need congressional term limits, transparency, limits to campaign contributions, accountability and clear restrictions on the gerrymandering of congressional districts. While we're at it, let's prevent Congressmen and women from naming bridges, roads and airports after themselves, or collecting a pension after they've been sentenced to prison for crimes they committed in office.

Fourth, the Framers could not have contemplated that our leaders in Washington could become so entrenched that they could bribe voters with the voters' own money, or with money stolen from the voters' children. The national debt roughly doubled under George W. Bush, and it doubled again under Barack Obama. That's a four-fold increase in only 16 years. It is lunacy to believe that this level of spending can be sustained. The national debt now stands at roughly 100% of gross national product. And that doesn't even come close to accounting for the federal government's unfunded liabilities and entitlements (for example, the federal government now guarantees the vast majority of new home mortgages—the lessons of the "Great Recession" are obviously unlearned). We need a constitutional limitation preventing intergenerational theft and imposing some basic level of fiscal responsibility.

Fifth, the Framers of the Constitution could not have contemplated that Congress would delegate unprecedented powers to administrative agencies, which themselves would employ influence over Congress, and further, that those administrative agencies would not themselves be subject to the Constitution's division of powers—executive, legislative, judicial— that keeps the rest of government in check. Today, we have administrative agencies that have run amok, with the power to make rules, enforce those rules, and adjudicate those rules. Not one of those administrative agencies is beholden to voters. Yes, yes, we need something like the FAA to control air traffic, the FDA to license new drugs, and the EPA to assure that the Cuyahoga river doesn't catch fire again. But we don't need imperious bureaucrats dictating to us which direction to wipe our ass.

Sixth, though the Framers of the Constitution all sought to put reigns on the powers of federal government, it apparently did not occur to them that depriving the government of the power to take a human life might be a good way to go about it. Regardless of that omission, today capital punishment is no longer a deterrence to crime, and it is a serious drain on the public purse. It's already prohibited in 19 states and the District of Columbia. It's time to make it go away for good.

Article V of the Constitution contemplates two means by which that document may be amended. Only one has been attempted, sometimes for noble purposes (abolition of slavery) and sometimes not (prohibition of alcohol). Congress meets, agrees on a proposed amendment, and then sends it on to the states for ratification.

The other way, never attempted, is for the states themselves to call a constitutional convention. "The Congress . . . on the Application of the Legislatures of two thirds of the several States, shall call a Convention for proposing Amendments, which . . . shall be valid to all Intents and Purposes, as part of this Constitution, when ratified by the Legislatures of three fourths of the several States." Meet, agree on one or more amendments, and send it/them off to the state legislatures for ratification. It's a way for the states to shove it right up the political elite's lower digestive tract, thereby giving us all an extra level of satisfaction.

Some people play fantasy football. I write fantasy constitutional amendments.

I will share with you just a few of them below, which are calculated to benefit the Republic and not ruffle the feathers of ideologues on either the right or the left.

****

Constitutional Amendments (side bar)
Proposed Amendment A: TERM LIMITS
Section 1.
No person shall be elected or appointed to the office of the House of Representatives more than six times.
Section 2.
No person shall be elected or appointed to the office of the Senate more than two times.

Section 3.

No person shall cumulatively serve more than twenty years as a judge in the federal judiciary.

Section 4.

This Amendment shall apply only prospectively to any sitting member, or to any previously elected or appointed member, of the House of Representatives, Senate or Judiciary.

Proposed Amendment B: RIGHT OF PRIVACY

The right of persons to be secure in the privacy of their communications, files, records, friendships, consensual adult sexual activities, personal and political associations, and treatments for sickness, disease or the prevention thereof, shall not be infringed.

Proposed Amendment C: DIRECT ELECTION OF PRESIDENT

Section 1.

The Electoral College is hereby abolished. The election of the President of the United States shall henceforth be made by direct, popular ballot conducted in a national election.

Section 2.

The selection of any political party's candidate for President of the United States shall be by direct, popular ballot conducted in one or more national primary elections. Any such primary election shall take place no more than 90, nor less than 30, days before the general election for President. No party may nominate a candidate for President unless and until such candidate receives a majority of votes cast in the primary election.

Proposed Amendment D: MAKING CONGRESS ACCOUNTABLE

Section 1.

Congress shall pass no law which shall exempt members of Congress from such law, or otherwise exclude members of Congress from its practical application.

Section 2.

Congress shall consider no amendment to proposed legislation which calls for the expenditure of public funds for the exclusive, or primary, benefit of a particular state or congressional district, or constituent(s) located therein.

Section 3.

No member of Congress shall enjoy immunity from prosecution for crimes committed, or immunity from civil liability by reason of actions which have occurred, during a duly convened session of Congress.

Section 4.

Neither the President, nor any member of Congress, nor any candidate for either office shall, directly or indirectly, accept remuneration, or a gift of more than token value, from any foreign government or person representing or advocating the interests thereof.

Section 5.

Neither the President, nor any member of Congress, nor any candidate for either office shall, directly or indirectly, accept remuneration, or a gift of more than token value, from any governmental office or administrative agency or person representing or advocating the interests thereof.

Section 6.

No project or item financed with public funds may be named after any sitting President or sitting member of Congress, and no project or item financed with public funds may be named after any former President or member of Congress who played a role in obtaining the financing for it.

Section 7.

No person shall, directly or indirectly, profit or otherwise derive personal benefit from the use of non-public information obtained by virtue of his or her position in, or with, Congress or the office of President.

Section 8.

Neither the President, nor any member of Congress shall, upon retirement from the office of President or Congress, receive a pension that exceeds the cumulative compensation that he or she received while serving in such capacity.

Section 9.

Neither the President, nor any member of Congress, shall receive remuneration of any kind upon their conviction of a high crime and misdemeanor committed while serving in such capacity.

Section 10.

The President, as the chief executive, shall faithfully execute all of the laws passed by Congress. It shall be an impeachable offense for the President to willfully refuse or fail to enforce a law, or any portion of a law, of Congress, or attempt to circumvent, negate or eviscerate such law by executive action or inaction.

Proposed Amendment E: SENSIBLE RULES ON SPENDING MONEY

Section 1.

No annual budget to finance the operations of the federal government shall exceed projected tax revenues, except in times of *bona fide* national emergency. Projections of tax revenues shall be based upon empirical data, compiled and derived impartially and in good faith.

Section 2.

In the event Congress and the President shall fail to reach agreement on an annual operating budget for the federal government, upon the expiration of the previously approved budget, neither the President, nor any member of

Congress, shall derive compensation for his or her service until a new budget is passed. No successive budget shall allow for the retroactive payment of compensation to either the President or to any member of Congress, nor shall it allow for an increase in compensation to either the President or to any member of Congress from that which was authorized in the most recently approved budget.

Section 3.

No continuing resolution to fund the operations of federal government in lieu of an annual budget shall be valid if it calls for the expenditure of funds in excess of the funds authorized by the most recently approved budget.

Proposed Amendment F: MAKING ADMINISTRATIVE AGENCIES ACCOUNTABLE TO THE PEOPLE

Section 1. Every federal administrative agency shall cease to exist ten years from the date of the enactment of this Amendment unless Congress shall, by a two-thirds majority of each house, vote to keep it in existence in the manner prescribed in Section 2 below. No new administrative agency may be established except upon the affirmative vote of a two-thirds majority of each house of Congress, in the manner prescribed in Section 2 below.

Section 2. Any vote to establish, or continue the existence of, an administrative agency shall be accompanied by new enabling legislation which shall: (a) define the purpose of such administrative agency; (b) clearly describe and circumscribe the powers of such administrative agency; (c) establish clear standards and procedures to assure that such administrative agency, in the exercise of those powers, does not impose burdens upon society which exceed the reasonably expected benefits to society; (d) establish clear and reasonable procedures to prevent the abuse of power or the waste of resources by such administrative agency; (e) assure the protection of rights of persons under this Constitution; and (f) provide a clear mechanism to assure continued accountability to, and oversight and control by, the Congress.

Section 3. The Supreme Court and the inferior federal courts established in this Constitution shall have the exclusive authority and jurisdiction to hear disputes involving the enactment of rules, or the actions taken to enforce rules, by any federal administrative agency. No federal administrative agency shall perform judicial functions with respect to its own rules and actions.

Section 4.

Neither the President, nor any member of Congress, nor any person serving in the administrative offices of either the President or Congress, nor any candidate for such offices shall, directly or indirectly, accept remuneration, or a gift of more than token value, from any governmental office or administrative agency or person representing or advocating the interests thereof.

Section 5.

Any administrative agency established, or which has had its existence continued, in accordance with the procedures of Sections 1 and 2 hereof, shall itself cease to exist ten years from the date of its establishment or renewal, unless Congress shall continue its existence in accordance with the procedures of Sections 1 and 2 hereof.

Section 6.

Any effort by Congress to circumvent this Amendment by enlarging the powers of an existing administrative agency shall be null and void.

Proposed Amendment G: AN END TO GERRYMANDERING

Section 1. Promptly upon the completion of each national census, the Supreme Court shall convene and approve, or when required by population changes redraw, the boundaries of congressional districts within the states. The Supreme Court may also redraw any congressional district which has previously been gerrymandered by a political party.

Section 2. In re-drawing such congressional districts, the Supreme Court shall attempt to enfranchise the maximum number of citizens living within such districts, without consideration to race, ethnicity, or party affiliation, with the objective of fostering competitive elections within such districts. The Supreme Court shall disregard non-citizens in its drawing of congressional districts.

Section 3. In re-drawing such congressional districts, the Supreme Court shall attempt to minimize the length of boundaries separating congressional districts, and, wherever practicable, not draw a congressional district boundary which divides a county, parish, municipality or other pre-existing political entity. In drawing boundaries, the Supreme Court shall also consider the convenience of the voters who live within them.

Proposed Amendment H: AN END TO CAPITAL PUNISHMENT

Capital punishment for crimes committed within the United States or any territory subject to its jurisdiction is hereby abolished.

Chapter 10. The Constitutional Addendum on Abortion

> "Curses on the law! Most of my fellow citizens are the sorry consequences of uncommitted abortions."
>
> —Karl Kraus

In 1973, the Supreme Court declared abortion (well, at least in the first trimester) to be a fundamental right. Today, lefties revere *Roe v. Wade*, and conservatives loathe it. Greg Garrison, who has successfully prosecuted criminals who received the death sentence, decries it as "murder." There's no issue which divides the left and the right so passionately.

Prior to 1973, abortion was not illegal in the United States. It was simply a matter that could be regulated, or outlawed, under state law. Many states, in fact, permitted it.

I believe *Roe v. Wade* to be untenable, not because I think abortion is wrong but because of the arbitrary means by which the Supreme Court pegged human "rights" to human gestation, dividing it into thirds. First trimester, abortion is exclusively in the woman's discretion. After that, the state had an interest and could weigh in.

There is no scientific basis for dividing human gestation in this fashion. Oh yes, the Supremes decreed "quickening," or the independent movement of the fetus, to be a momentous stage in fetal development. "Quickening" happens to occur at the end of the first trimester, more or less. Not one of the Justices had a background in science or medicine, as I recall.

Any way you cut it, the first trimester is arbitrary. The Justices selected it, no doubt, because of "quickening" and the fact that fetuses take on some human characteristics visible to the naked eye at its conclusion.

But as long as you don't buy into the notion that life begins at conception, things inevitably get messy. It's a seamless process of cell division that begins with one fertilized cell, and ends with a baby. Not one of the lefties wants, even today, to actually define the moment when human life begins during pregnancy. They gloss over the tri-partite division the Justices created for us in 1973, and hope that the conservatives will continue to be too obtuse to see the flaw.

Meanwhile, under tort law, we allow recovery for fetal injury and death caused by the negligent or intentional acts of another. "Messy" doesn't begin to describe this conundrum.

Science has made much progress since 1973 and continues to make progress. We've pushed back the gestation period where a baby may survive out of the womb well into the second trimester. At some point, that Rubicon will be crossed. Maybe someday we'll be able to grow babies without the help of a uterus at all.

So herein lies the problem. A great many people want abortion on demand, but none of them wants to be labeled a murderer. A good part of the abortion debate, one that continues to divide our country so starkly, can be boiled down to semantics.

It's time we had a grown-up conversation.

We kill people every day. Our military exists for the purpose of killing people. We execute prisoners convicted of capital crimes, and in some places we assist people who wish to commit suicide. Nearly every Will I have drafted contains a clause appointing a health care representative with instructions not to prolong life unnecessarily.

Each year, American cops kill about 1,000 citizens they are supposed to be protecting. Citizens kill each other in far greater numbers. We kill ourselves a lot, too. About half of the people in the US who are labeled "victims of gun violence" have actually turned the barrel on themselves. (In this respect, guns do a lot less "violence" than we give credit, and there'd be a lot of messy sidewalks without them.) We share more than 98% of our genes in common with chimpanzees, yet we use them for medical experiments in procedures which kill them, too.

We kill. Get over it.

So let's get used to the idea that a woman can cut a fetus out of her own body, regardless of what we might call it. If you don't like abortion, don't get one.

In my discussions with my conservative friends like Greg Garrison, they never fail to mention the "sanctity of life." They utter these words with such reverence and finality that I must pursue an entirely new tack. (They invariably never share such empathy for prisoners on death row, by the way.) I query, "So who's being aborted"?

It turns out that the vast majority of abortions are to single women who can't afford, or don't want, a baby at this time of life. A much higher percentage of them are non-white than the population at large. Redneck Reds erroneously think that if these women are compelled to carry their babies to term, they will automatically morph into the doting mothers you see at the YMCA and begin attending church on Sundays. Unfortunately, this isn't remotely true and these unwanted and often abused kids grow up in harsh environments where they are neither loved nor wanted, and consequently develop socialization issues, dropping out of school, etc.

Statisticians and demographers have thus theorized that the remarkable drop in our country's crime rate in the last generation can be attributed in no small part to *Roe v. Wade*. John J. Donohue and Steven D. Levitt published this theory in 2001, and despite its rebarbative implications, the facts seem to bear them out. We are, in a word, aborting future Bruised Blues.

24. People used to have a lot more kids

The anti-abortion billboards which dot Kentuckiana inevitably depict a cherubic blond-haired, blue-eyed baby that's about to be tossed into a wood-chipper. It's calculated to look like a Scotch-Irish version of the Christ-child and to tug on the heart-strings of church-going white people. But that's not the poster-child for an aborted fetus, even in Kentuckiana.

Chapter 11. The "Flynn Effect" and "Moore's Law"

> "The difference between stupidity and genius is that genius has its limits".

—Albert Einstein

In a recent YouGov poll, 96% of Americans surveyed believed themselves to be at or above-average intelligence. I regard this poll to be confirmation of American Exceptionalism. In some places in America, like Lake Wobegon, Minnesota, every single one of the children is above average. Jasper, Indiana, is a place like that, too.

Three decades ago, a researcher at the University of Otago (New Zealand) by the name of James R. Flynn examined intelligence test data from over two dozen countries, and observed IQ test scores to be rising across the board at a steady rate of 0.3 point/year. Flynn's findings have since been confirmed by numerous follow-up studies, using test data from every inhabited continent that goes back to the beginning of the 20th century. In this manner, the term "Flynn Effect" was born.

The cumulative effect of such an increase in brain power will have far-reaching consequences for the human race: Someday, "Beyond the Wormhole" hosted by Morgan Freeman will have more viewers than "Dancing with the Stars." We may even be compelled to retire "Village Idiot" accolades at the Story Inn by the beginning of the 24th century, as Captain Jean Luc Picard takes the helm of the Enterprise.

According to the better-known "Moore's Law," computing power doubles, on average, every 18 months or so, and this has been going on since the 1970s. Due to the power of geometric increase, computers will soon overtake our intelligence, despite our considerable head-start. With luck, we'll develop a symbiosis with computers before they wake up and eradicate us as pests.

It was with the assistance of a benevolent computer that humans were able to catch Fareed Zakaria in his first act of plagiarism, conduct which would have merited his expulsion from a reputable newspaper. But at *TIME* Magazine, his dirty deed earned him a mere 30-day suspension (upon investigating the matter, *TIME* was satisfied that his copying of an entire paragraph from an article published in the *New Yorker* was "unintentional"). He kept his job at CNN, too. Regardless, we may now add "unoriginal" to the adjectives "unimaginative," "hackneyed," "didactic" and "shallow" when describing Zakaria's writings.

Indeed, *TIME's* diminishing subscribership itself may be anecdotal confirmation of the "Flynn Effect." A smarter, better educated and more literate population craves something of real substance to read, like *The Economist*. But clearly, the benefits of the "Flynn Effect" have not been evenly distributed throughout the population, and certainly have not penetrated all parts of the "new economy." Both publishing and investment banking have little to show for it. Witness Time-Warner's disastrous merger a few years ago with AOL, a dial-up online service that had never even once turned a profit. Apparently, the brain-trust behind that move expected to make up for the losses in higher volume. AT&T's acquisition years later made more sense, motivated as it was to pad the bottom line by stifling competition.

A few years ago I had the life-enriching experience of joining Butler University faculty sitting with Zakaria's boss, Richard A. Stengel, at the annual commencement ceremony. I was there to hand a diploma to my son Rich, a real pleasure. In addressing the Butler graduates, Stengel heaped praise on Zakaria, just as he was about to commit his act of . . . uh . . . unintentional copying. (Butler declined to allow Chief Justice John Roberts to speak at an earlier commencement, declaring him to be "too controversial." Add university administrators to those yet untouched by the "Flynn Effect.")

Unpunished and undeterred, Zakaria went on to borrow heavily from other authors in the years that followed. Such is the sorry state of American journalism. Recall the media frenzy over the gang rape that didn't occur at the Phi Kappa Psi house at the University of Virginia.

The rape story's utter contempt for fact did not deter *Rolling Stone* from publishing it, inciting a gaggle of sanctimonious students and faculty to mob the fraternity house demanding swift retribution from its occupants. Now that the story's been exposed as a fraud, its author/propagandist, Sabrina Rubin Erdely, has apologized to "Rolling Stone's readers, to my Rolling Stone editors and colleagues, to the UVA community, and to any victims of sexual assault who may feel fearful as a result of my article." Notably, she did NOT apologize to the seven boys she falsely accused of felonious behavior.

College campuses are hardly bastions of free speech these days. Penn State University, defrocked of its football titles for suppressing news of shower-room hijinks that would have made Fr. Goeghan blush, recently felt compelled to designate a "free speech zone" on its campus, a tacit acknowledgment that First Amendment rights have been effectively suspended there (except as might be tolerated by the PSU administration). Such is the compulsion to assure cultural inclusivity and political correctness in the hallowed halls of academe.

In an open letter, faculty at my own alma mater, Duke University, hastily denounced another gang rape that didn't take place on its campus in 2006, this time by members of the lily-white lacrosse team. Prosecutor Michael Nifong was eventually disbarred for pursuing that case after he learned it to be a fraud, but the esteemed Duke faculty members who libeled those boys suffered no consequences at all. No sign of the "Flynn Effect" there.

The University of California has concluded that it is racist micro-aggression to suggest that America is the "land of opportunity." That's because, by implication, if you fail at a task, it implies that you have your only yourself to blame.

Donald Trump is not much encumbered by facts or information. He would do well to read and listen more and talk less. But his railings about "media bias" have more than a kernel of truth to them. Zakaria's buddy at CNN, Donna Brazile, fed questions to the Clinton campaign before a presidential debate. She was fired (i.e., thrown under the bus) when she was caught, so as not to tarnish the CNN brand. While Brazile was the deputy national field director for Michael Dukakis in the late 1980s, she knowingly planted and/or fanned a false rumor that George W. Bush had had an extramarital affair. When she was caught committing that fraud, Dukakis threw her under the bus, too. I struggle to believe that Brazile was caught each of the only two times she spread misinformation for the benefit of Progressive causes, and would cynically note that her obvious bias did not hurt her career as a "journalist." Brazile's partisanship eventually earned her a promotion to Chair of the Democratic National Committee, where she can finally abandon any pretense of objectivity.

Like Brazile, George Stephanopoulos worked on the Dukakis campaign. Stephanopoulos is now the Chief Political Correspondent for that monument to objectivity, ABC News. He called for Trump's "impeachment" even *before* he had been sworn in as President.

"Journalist" Glenn Thrush was busted by WikiLeaks for sending his election coverage stories to Clinton's staffers for their "approval," famously writing: "Please don't share or tell anyone I did this. Tell me if I [messed] up anything." His dishonesty earned him a promotion to White House Correspondent for *The New York Times*.

TIME's twin sister *Newsweek* published 125,000 copies of a commemorative edition flatteringly entitled "Madam President," even before the polls had opened on November 8, 2016. It hastily recalled them on November 9, though a few scattered copies escaped. These are now in high demand among collectors, selling for several times the original $10.95 newsstand price. I'd love to get my hands on that "Dewey Defeats Truman" paper as well.

As mainstream media has drifted left, "new media" has drifted right. It is a matter of gospel on the right that "climate change" is a hoax, and the push to "renewable energy" is a left-wing conspiracy to kill coal-mining jobs in Kentuckiana and keep us from leaving home. Even the most blinded conspiracy theorists would be hard-pressed to believe that Hillary Clinton and John Podesta were operating a child sex abuse ring from the back of a Washington, DC pizza shop. Stephen Bannon of Breitbart "News" steered traffic to his website with "click bait" and occasional fake news. His success as a propagandist has earned him a job as Trump's chief strategist. Even somewhat respectable news websites routinely carry "sponsored" material that could easily be mistaken as real news.

Whether this nonsense is a reaction to the prevailing culture of Progressivism or not is a matter of conjecture. We humans have evolved to be news hunters and gatherers, not news sifters, and this deluge of un-digestible drivel from both right and left is doing us lasting harm.

"Progressivism" has all of the intolerance and stale dogma that characterizes a religion. College campuses serve as its place of worship, faculty serve as its high priests, and journalists as its missionaries. There is no evidence whatsoever that the "Flynn Effect" is improving things.

Scientists are puzzled just how the "Flynn Effect" came to be. I have a theory, one that will assure that I am tarred and feathered on college campuses, thereby giving it some level of credibility.

Now that we have mapped the human genome and accumulated decades of empirical data, no one can deny the heritability of intelligence, no matter how predisposed one might be to the politically correct proposition that nurture always trumps nature. (Even Zakaria would be loath to suppress this fact, regardless of whether it was published first in the *New Yorker*.)

Human females, being creatures of limited reproductive opportunity and unmatched intuition (some would be so sexist to call it "guile"), will necessarily strive to maximize the inclusive fitness of their offspring, even if it comes at the cruel expense of their putative partners. As Mark Twain said:

"A woman's intuition is better than a man's. Nobody knows anything, really, you know, and a woman can guess a good deal nearer than a man."

A British study in the 1950s determined that approximately 10% of births to married women were NOT the offspring of their husbands. This embarrassing fact has been confirmed by studies numerous times since, in many different cultures.

Clearly, human females prefer more intelligent and successful Alpha males to their own dullard partners, even if it condemns them to a genetic dead-end. The Alpha males out there are only too happy to oblige. In this manner, the gene pool of our race is continually enriched by the likes of John Edwards and Jesse Jackson, and cumulatively, we have the "Flynn Effect."

Sex researchers note that men consistently report about twice as many lifetime sex partners as women. Since the vast majority of sexual contacts occur between men and women, this makes no sense on its face.

It turns out that women are mostly responsible for this discrepancy. When the studies are cloaked in anonymity, women report a much higher number of partners (though still slightly fewer, on average, than men).

It appears that our race is the product of surreptitious matings, and we have the brains to show for it.

CHAPTER 12. THE ARTS AND THE MUSIC

"What is art? Nature concentrated."

—Balzac, 1799–1850

Brown County is a wild, bucolic place on the doorstep of Indiana University. Its Jacobs School of Music is world-class. So is every other department remotely related to the arts. Even IU's Law School produced a brilliant musician: Hoagy Carmichael. If Kentuckiana is ever to become a state, "Stardust" should be its state song.

It should come as no surprise that some of that considerable talent should come to rest here in Brown County.

Artists discovered the beauty of Brown County a long time ago. Painter T.C. Steele did his greatest work here, after his stint in Europe studying Impressionism. The locals were suspicious, and jealous, of him because of his player-piano.

Steele's home and studio are now a museum that is well worth visiting (several of his very valuable paintings hang in IU's Student Union building). The TC Steele Museum is located about five miles from Story, as the crow flies. (Unfortunately, the road between Story and the Museum was severed in 1960, with the flooding of the town of Elkinsville, so one must drive there by a more circuitous route.)

Photographer Frank Hohenberger did his best work here, too. Despite ponderously slow shutter speeds and primitive black and white film, he captured forever the faces, life and times of the hardscrabble settlers of Brown County. His classic photographs speak volumes, many of which illustrate this book.

Contemporary landscape photographer Gary Moore has captured the ineffable rustic beauty of this place in his book, "Brown County Mornings."

Some years back, local artist Luke Buck created an iconic watercolor of the front of the General Store at Story, which nearby Oliver Winery briefly used to label a wine bottle. The last four of Luke's numbered watercolors are now framed and displayed at the Story Inn. They are, most emphatically, not for sale.

25. The folks in the holler did better making moonshine.

Cartoonist Kin Hubbard made a career of lampooning the people who lived here, which he could do from the relative safety of Indianapolis. But even in his most vitriolic moments, he revered Brown County's raw beauty and rustic charm, an inspiration to artists of every ilk.

26. *Adding value, after commodity prices tanked.*

Although John Mellencamp is not, strictly speaking, a Brown County resident, it is not implausible to call him a native son. His mother Marilyn ran an art studio here at the Story Inn with Ole and Joan Olson until a couple of years ago. Marilyn and Joan are both oil painters of no mean talent. John displayed his paintings here a few years ago. Very few people know that John Mellencamp is a painter, too, and a very good one.

The writings of Kurt Vonnegut, a German Freidenker from Indianapolis, still resonate among the literate people of Kentuckiana. His grandfather, Bernard Vonnegut, was the architect in 1894 who designed *Das Deutsche Haus* in Indianapolis (re-named the Athenaeum in 1918). This magnificent 80,000 square ft. brick and slate Renaissance Revival building was a monument to art, athleticism, alcohol and secularism. It still serves that role today.

I strived mightily to save that building from the wrecking ball from 1991–4, when the forces of entropy and the laws of economics conspired to make the land under that building more valuable than the building itself. Far more than a building was at stake. Generations of Hoosiers, including Vonnegut, have ties to that temple. I will go to my grave convinced that preserving this structure from demolition was one of my more significant accomplishments as a lawyer.

It was through the Athenaeum that I met Frank Mueller, and the Athenaeum served as inspiration for our purchasing the town of Story in 1999. "One more for the Gipper," I told him.

Author James Alexander Thom and his lovely Native-American wife Dark Rain are Brown County residents too, and sometimes visitors to the Story Inn. They have written extensively about life in Kentuckiana at the dawn of European migration. *The Red Heart* is a favorite book of mine.

27. No one here's wearing Prada.

Ruth Reichmann's a Brown County native as well. She, her late husband Eberhard, and a colleague in Indianapolis named Giles Hoyt, have worked and written tirelessly to connect Hoosiers with their German roots.

Ruth is a vanishing breed of German-Jew. It comes as a surprise to many that Germans on this side of the Atlantic, particularly those who migrated in 1848 escaping the religious idiocy that tore the fabric of life in Europe, did not draw a line between Christians and Jews. German-Americans were staunch abolitionists before and during the Civil War, and their descendants (among them Kurt Vonnegut) eagerly served in the American armed forces to defeat the Nazis in World War II.

Herein lies another example of something I do not understand. A German-Jew who becomes a Freidenker is still Jewish. But a German-Catholic who becomes a Freidenker is no longer Catholic. Query: If a German-Catholic first converts to Judaism, and then thinks the better of it and becomes a Freidenker, can he still lay claim to being Jewish? And will that brief interlude confer upon him the remarkable ability to compose a happy tune in the minor key?

As a Freidenker who suffered through the apocalyptic Allied bombing of Dresden as an American POW and later lived among Jews and connected with Christ, Vonnegut could perhaps only communicate effectively in the genre of science fiction. In a way, he was just a time-travel writer.

Brown County has inspired musicians for generations. Mellencamp is only the most famous. We even have our own musical genre, called "Kentuckiana," a blend of Folk, Rock and Bluegrass. Bill Monroe, who has a park here that bears his name, was one of the world's most famous Bluegrass musicians. Bluegrass music, of course, has Celtic roots, and it is one cultural nugget that I have been able to swallow without indigestion. Bluegrass/Kentuckiana Music is what we play at the Indiana Wine Fair.

The list goes on and on.

For more than 15 years, we've had chamber musicians perform in the Story Inn's restaurant. The vast bulk of them were here to pursue advanced degrees, and move on. Musicians need to eat like everyone else, and so it was an easy fit.

German violinist David Yonan played his Stradivarius here, performing Mozart as well as some of his own compositions (caveat: David did not attend IU). David, also a German-Jew, is perhaps Europe's top violinist, and has performed at Carnegie Hall and other places much better known than the Story Inn. These days, he hangs out at the University of Chicago, and occasionally drops by.

One evening, David treated Jane and me to a solo performance with his Stradivarius. He played Schubert, Mozart and Stravinsky, in the Carriage House. Kings, popes and emperors should be so blessed.

Russian violinist Matvey Lapin played here, too, with his charming pianist companion Katya Kramer. I watched Katya earn her Master's Degree by performing a Rachmaninoff concerto, 10,000 keystrokes *in toto*, without sheet music, flawlessly. She did an even better job here at Story, under the influence of wine. The couple was eventually married here, and they now have two children who carry their rich blood lines.

Violists Ben and Jenny Weiss performed here, too, before moving to Charleston to become anchors of the Spoleto festival. On October 6, 2005, we did a "Mozart on the Meadow" to celebrate German-American Day. Ben, Jenny and several other musicians donned full 19th century costume. One afternoon performance included a breathtaking display by two Lipizzaners in the field.

Some years back, we had a charming quartet of Taiwanese musicians, which we dubbed the "East Side Story." (They understood the cultural nuances of that name as well as I did. I returned the favor by never subjecting them to the indignity of calling them "Chinese".) Currently, we have a concert pianist, Ted Seaman, from Cincinnati. Ted plays Hoagy Carmichael as well as the classics from composers of my era, 18th century Europe.

Brown County is richly endowed with sculptors, painters, musicians, photographers, writers, winemakers and artists of every ilk. Previously, the Brown County Convention Visitor's Bureau called us the "Art Colony of the Midwest." That was hyperbole, but barely.

One of my good friends, Brad Cox, is an artisan welder. Brad can take a piece of scrap metal and turn it into a functioning artwork that would make Michelangelo proud. He's provided us with numerous accouterments here at Story, including a bike rack made from old railings, bar stools fashioned from old tractor seats, and the world's most unusual meat-smoker. (Brad becomes animated, incidentally, after just three beers.)

The hills and hollers of Brown County are populated with artists, even those who possess no artistic talent. I'm one of them. I fancy myself to be a restauranteur, even though I am challenged to microwave a hot dog.

The Brown County Art Gallery in Nashville is a wonderful place to visit, both to see what's on display and to obtain brochures which will direct you to functioning art galleries around the county. In the summer, you can take a leisurely, loosely guided tour called the "Studio Garden Tour." Two miles east of Story is Spears Gallery, where Larry Spears fires up his kiln to create some of the loveliest clay pots and mugs you will find this side of Eden.

It has been said that there's no art in money, and no money in art. From my observation, the top artists in Brown County are not candidates for the Forbes 100. But it's taken me a while to recognize that money is not necessarily the pursuit of artists, here or anywhere.

I am not wealthy either, but I fancy myself to be a minor player, like a lesser (but still pretentious) 18th century European noble who mentors and cultivates people with talent by inviting them to court, providing a stipend, and letting them dine for free.

CHAPTER 13. THE ROADS AND TRAILS LESS TRAVELED

> "I have found out there ain't no surer way
> to find out whether you like people or hate
> them than to travel with them."
> —Tom Sawyer

Unless you travel to Story by foot, you'll need horsepower of one kind or another, or a bicycle. In some respects, getting here can be half the fun.

Story sits at the end of the "E" Trail of the Brown County State Park, connecting it to the largest horseman's camp in the Midwest.

Some years ago, Edward O. Wilson of Harvard advanced the "Biophilia" hypothesis. Very simply, Biophilia is an instinctive bond between humans and other living systems. Wilson described it as the "urge to affiliate with other forms of life." We have pets and house plants, visit zoos and national parks, and by instinct are driven to see Nature as a thing of beauty.

To me, Biophilia seemed as self-evident as Newton's force of "gravity." Humans form bonds with other living things, and those attachments can be very strong. Just ask a horseman. Scientists get credit, sometimes, just for stating the obvious.

Keeping a horse is not cheap or easy. They have little value for work or transport these days. They eat a lot, discharge prodigious amounts of solid, liquid and gaseous waste products, and need a pasture for turn-out. That makes it impossible to own one in a city. And though horses are big and strong and appear to be indestructible to us, they are in fact quite fragile creatures. One slip and fall can lame them for a season, or for life. One slip and fall can kill you, too, if you happen to land underneath the beast when it goes down.

These detractions do not deter thousands of equine lovers from converging upon the Brown County State Park's Horseman's Camp each year, beginning roughly at the time the snows melt for good. These horsemen pitch a tent, saddle up, and explore upwards of 50 miles of trails through wilderness at a plodding three miles per hour or so. At the end of the "E" Trail, which is but one of many such trails in the park, is a fine tavern. Horsemen tend to drink a lot, so that's quite a gravitational pull.

Now, I cannot understate the cultural chasm that exists between the trail riders we get in Brown County and the equestrian culture that we find in Bluegrass country south of the Ohio River, where they raise steeds for speed. The Kentucky Derby is bluegrass country's marquis event, and it is, unambiguously, a race. Trail riders do not race. Jockeys abstain from alcohol until the race is over. Trail riders drink before, during and after their ride. People pay to watch horses race and bet on the outcome. No one cares to watch horsemen ambling along a trail, and there's no outcome that merits placing a wager. But both activities do involve horses as well as the consumption of alcohol, which might describe everything they have in common.

Trail riding also has nothing in common with dressage, an odd sport in which overgrown adolescent girls with rich older husbands seek to become emotionally fulfilled by forcing their geldings to dance to baroque music. I find baroque music to be delightful, especially when drinking a nice wine. But it is undignified to compel a horse to dance to it. Some dressage riders don't even drink. (Ann Romney, for example, is a teetotaler.) I don't understand the sport, but then again, there are a lot of things I do not understand. Things like why there are no Hispanic-looking people on Mexican television, or why a small rural police department in Kentuckiana would ever need an armored personnel carrier.

On a typical Saturday afternoon in nice weather, upwards of 200 horses will make the trek to Story from camp, each carrying a thirsty cowboy or cowgirl. They generally arrive about lunchtime and saddle back up about two hours later after consuming a hamburger and a few shots of "Jack" or "Jim." Horses can see in the dark quite well, but their riders cannot, and thus most horsemen prefer to ride by daylight. Besides, there's a fire to build, and more whiskey to drink, back at camp. The tavern quiets down a little after 4pm.

In the Story Inn's rustic subterranean tavern, which dates back to the original store, circa 1870s, the bar tops are made of old barn wood. The tables are cut from the lanes of an old bowling alley. The bar stools are old tractor seats, and bare lightbulbs hang from a low tin ceiling, low enough to be taken out by a Stetson. The bar has a full complement of fine wines, beers and spirits, but the horsemen eschew such beverages to slake their thirst with whiskey. By the time the early dinner crowd begins to arrive, wearing

Birkenstocks and loose-fitting khakis, to sip a Willamette Valley Pinot Noir as an *aperitif*, the rowdy horsemen have already hit the trail.

Overall, it is much safer to ride a horse under the influence of alcohol than it is to drive a motorized vehicle with the same degree of impairment, for the simple reason that horses, in many respects, are much smarter than humans. They have an uncanny sense of direction, far better than any GPS, and never stray from the shortest practicable route back to camp. And, unlike a vehicle, horses possess a genuine desire to get themselves, and their passengers, there safely. That's Biophilia.

When it comes to trail riding, I am a neophyte. But at least I've done enough of it to appreciate its fascination. I remember fondly taking a ride on the back of a curmudgeonly old gelded American Quarterhorse by the name of Puck, as I was recovering from foot surgery. I couldn't walk, but Puck was happy to do the walking for me. And on a crisp, clear autumn day, high up on his back, it seemed that I could see for miles. It was made all that more enjoyable by the fact that Puck provided a heated seat, and at my advanced age, I consider a heated seat to be a necessity when traveling. I had no desire to move faster than a slow walk, and so Puck and I got along just fine.

Some years back, the Queen of England attended the Kentucky Derby. We tuned into the race on the town's only television, which happens to be in the tavern. The horsemen visiting Story that day watched the race with interest only because some of them had wagered on it. Not one of them gave a hoot that the Queen was in attendance.

To the south and west of Story lies the Hoosier National Forest, a true wilderness to traverse on horseback. Some brave souls embark on a two-day, sixty-mile ride that originates at Midwest Trail Ride Outpost in Norman, Indiana, to Story, and then back. This route is far less traveled, and more challenging by orders of magnitude, than the "E" Trail from the park. It should not be attempted without an experienced guide and a commitment to drinking in moderation.

When these intrepid travelers arrive at Story, we put up their horses. We're a B&B for horses, too. The horsemen, meanwhile, have a shower and a steak. In the morning, we feed the humans breakfast and pack them a lunch for the return trip.

Before embarking on a trip to Brown County by motorized vehicle, it's important to understand the peculiar road conditions that prevail there. There's only one road in and out of Story: State Road 135. Story sits at the junction of SR135 and Elkinsville Road, a county road which dead-ends five miles to the west. Nowhere is the poor quality of county road and bridge maintenance more in evidence than at this junction. The state road is smooth and paved; the county road looks like London after the *Blitzkrieg*. There's no pretense of paving Elkinsville Road at all two miles beyond Story.

In my humble opinion, SR 135 is one of Kentuckiana's most scenic byways, taking you past covered bridges, clapboard churches, weather-beaten barns, wind-swept cemeteries, and fine fall foliage. Yes, the road is curvy, poorly banked, narrow, lacking in guard rails and, in some places, bermless. But compared to the county roads, SR 135 looks like the Autobahn. The county roads are a disgrace, navigable only by off-road vehicles, pick-up trucks, Jeeps and military vehicles. Fortunately, it is possible to travel Brown County and completely avoid them.

This makes driving either a challenge or a joy, depending upon your perspective. I briefly yielded to the desire to own a BMW convertible (yes, a red two-seater with leather seats—can you say "mid-life crisis"?), and thereby discovered the meaning of the word *"Fahrvergnügen."* One often sees a high-performance car, or a classic garage queen, in the Story Inn's parking lot.

In good weather, we host a car club almost every weekend. Model-Ts, Jeeps, Mustangs, Austin-Healeys, hot rods, etc. They arrive in slow-moving columns, and the owners spend a good 30 minutes or so in the parking lot swapping stories before having a group lunch, and then they're off again. Frequently, they'll pause in front of the General Store for a picture. These groups almost never drink alcohol. Many of them are susceptible to having a stroke if it rains.

Owning an antique car is a lot like owning a horse. They're useless as a form of transportation, but fun to ride. Briefly, I owned a 1950 Ford as well, but yielded it to make room in the garage for kids' bikes. (Furthermore, it didn't have a heated seat.)

When it comes to commitment to an arcane form of travel, one group stands out from all the others: Harley riders.

America's fascination with Harleys is one concept that I cannot grasp. But there are a lot of things in this world I do not understand. Things like why women cannot set a thermostat or read a map. Or why DirecTV won't let us buy just the satellite channels we want for the television in the tavern. Maybe it has something to do with the fact that DirecTV is a subsidiary of AT&T.

Actually, I cannot even fathom why someone would willingly sit on an inherently unstable two-wheeled vehicle and drive it anywhere. This puts Harley riders in company with bikers of every other ilk, including those who pilot stealthy BMWs. Four wheels = good. Two wheels = bad.

Take away the civilizing influences of a muffler and a helmet, add some tattoos and leathers and a Rebel flag to make you look like a Klingon, put a cigarette in your mouth, and you have my vision of pure hell. Dante himself couldn't have concocted more loathsome scene of torture.

Put me on the seat of a Harley with resonating side-pipes, clad in black leathers in the scorching summer heat, with the sun piercing my already thin hair to create spots of melanoma on my scalp as it cooks what is left of my brain. That would define for me the meaning of "cruel and unusual punishment." Do that to me, and I'll confess to any crime.

Except for the occasional sound of gunfire, which is mostly friendly, the country is a quiet place. That's what makes it a nice place to visit. No sirens, no jackhammers, no boom boxes, no wheezing busses. Yet there is this dedicated cross section of society that is determined to shatter that bucolic scene, not just for themselves but for everyone else around them.

As an 18th century liberal, I would not ordinarily complain when someone takes to the road on a two-wheeled vehicle without first donning a helmet. It's an evolutionary feedback loop, culling those who are unfit to breed anyway. Add to that the bonus of harvesting some extra organs, and there are some compelling reasons declare helmet-less driving to be a basic American right to be enshrined in the Constitution.

Unfortunately, it is society which inevitably picks up the tab for brain injuries which could have been prevented by wearing a helmet. People like Jane Ammeson would be aghast to think that Harley riders should bear the consequences of their own poor judgment. Ergo, I am persuaded that helmet laws are, on balance, good things.

Like the horsemen, the Harley riders make a bee-line for the tavern, where they will predictably order a burger or BBQ and a beer. Sometimes two beers. We limit them to two beers, for obvious reasons. There are only two brands of beer that Harley riders will order: Bud Light, or Miller Lite. It makes restocking easy.

Harley Riders and horsemen share a palate for smoked pork, and at Story, we have the mother of all smokers. It's a converted 250 gallon liquid propane tank, painted black, with an old firebox to pump heat into it. The smoker looks like a cross between a submarine and a steam-punk still, since it is adorned with decorative copper tubing, superfluous dials and wheels, and faux legs from an old Singer sewing machine. Though "Big Doc" looks to be a creation of Jules Verne, our former Town Manager Kevin Allen designed him and welder-artist Brad Cox actually built him.

"Big Doc" took seven burly guys to set in place, and he now permanently rests under a rain shelter cobbled together from the pieces of a derelict barn, right next to a large grill where we often finish the job he started. We fire up "Big Doc," and his companion grill, on warm weekends to allow the aroma of pulled pork to draw cowboys the way a bug-light will attract mosquitoes.

I have discovered "Big Doc" to have an additional, unexpected quality. He's an irresistible attractant of heterosexual men, who gather around him to relive and embellish hunting stories. Stomach muscles inevitably relax, and with beer in hand they regale of life on the knife's edge of survival, where the only thing separating them from a fleeing doe was a 12-gauge shotgun, a bowie knife, and a side-arm. Every heterosexual man is an expert on killing, smoking and grilling meat.

To their credit, Harley riders and horsemen tip very well. They have been mixing at the Story Inn for a very long time, never with a violent incident. And Harley riders, like the horsemen, are usually gone by the time the Birkenstock crowd arrives, sparing us the embarrassment of having the "N" word uttered in the presence of someone who might find that to be offensive.

The lousy county roads and the proliferation of rutted, non-sanctioned paths which traverse the Hoosier National Forest bring out another, even less auspicious, motorist: the aficionado of off-road roading. These are typically gaunt, shirtless, tattooed cretins with bad teeth who customize old pick-up trucks with oversized tires so that they may ride over logs, through bogs, and flatten slow-moving animals. Customization always involves removing the muffler or anything else that might even slightly suppress engine noise.

28. *The county roads are not much better today.*

Unfortunately, they way they alter their vehicles, they create something that is inherently unstable, so they flip over a lot. Seat belts are *verboten*, as are helmets, so injuries are both predictable and common. The substantial alteration voids any manufacturer's warranty and nullifies any Section 402 (A) product liability claim, so once again, the taxpayers are left to pick up the hospital tab.

The quietest group to travel to Story, oddly enough, also arrives on two wheels. They are the bikers who get there by the power of human muscle. These are extreme athletes, with less than 3% body fat, who arrive with a powerful thirst as a consequence of physical exertion. Most of these are possessed of three-digit IQs, as evidenced by their bright clothing and helmets, and gustatory preferences.

The athlete-bikers may be divided into two groups: mountain bikers and road bikers. The former seek adventure by recklessly piloting their squat-looking bikes over fallen logs and rocky creek beds; the latter seek adventure by recklessly piloting their full-sized carbon-fiber bikes over berm-less, potholed country roads in competition with impaired, uninsured Brown County natives driving dented pick-up trucks. Other than this small detail, these two groups of athlete bikers are difficult to distinguish, except that if you observe that they are bleeding, they are almost always of the mountain biking variety. Road bikers' injuries are usually more serious, requiring transportation to a hospital, so they rarely visit us after they have been injured.

Like the Harley riders and the horsemen, these bikers seek out the tavern. But they arrive a lot later than the Harley-horsemen crowd, to keep company with the Birkenstock crowd becoming lubricated before their dinner table is ready upstairs. The athlete-bikers stay downstairs to eat, undoubtedly because they badly need to shower. To their credit, they recognize the necessity of showering.

The athlete-bikers' diet is far more diverse than either Harley riders' or horsemen's and includes such delicacies as seasonal salad, local cheese and charcuterie, pan-fried trout, Indiana duck, and, of course, rare beef filet. They inevitably indulge in beer, always, always, always choosing one of the locally crafted beers or ales, preferably on tap. If I ever witness an athlete-biker order a Bud Light, my software about all of humanity will have to be re-written.

PART II: WANDERLUST: JOURNEYS WITH JANE

Chapter 14. The Southwest

> "Some beautiful paths can't be discovered
> without getting lost." — Erol Ozan

For 16 years, I've indulged in a twice-weekly furlough, one that allows me to leave the Story Inn for a few hours and visit Indianapolis. It's part of my compensation package from Butler University, where I serve as an adjunct faculty member of the College of Business Administration. Except for those trips to "The City," I didn't get out much at all.

At least, that is, until I met Jane Simon Ammeson. Jane had a chat with my imaginary parole officer, and cautiously, I stepped out of Brown County to explore the rest of Kentuckiana with her.

At first, these trips were full of anxieties, as I found all manner of pretexts to call the front desk. "Is everything all right?" "Call me if you need something from Menards." (My car, inexplicably, will pull into the Menards parking lot and shut itself off for a good 15 minutes or so, leaving me no choice but to go inside and save big money.) I was a nervous parent checking in with the babysitter. But gradually, the trips with Jane became less stressful, and eventually, enjoyable.

Our journeys generally involved excursions to destinations that can be reached in three hours or less, for dinner and an overnight stay. To the south and west lie a considerable number of attractions, including Indiana's most enduring historic landmark, the West Baden Springs Hotel, and it's not so twin but still lovely sister, the French Lick Springs Resort Hotel, both in Orange County.

These two grand hotels were both founded on a failed business model: accommodating rich and famous patrons who would flock from places important, like Chicago and New York, to places unimportant and accessible only by rail, like French Lick. The country is dotted with such grand hotels. My favorite one is located in Bretton Woods, New Hampshire, famous for being the location of the conference that gave birth to the International Monetary Fund at the end of World War II.

Many of these grand hotels sought to model themselves after famous spas in Europe, and indeed, West Baden even copies the name "Baden-Baden," in Germany. The peculiar attraction here happened to be a malodorous creek full of sodium, lithium salts, magnesium sulfate and sulfur. It is so toxic that consuming just one cup of it will quickly cause cramping and diarrhea. Amazingly, people actually fell for this snake oil's putative curative properties. For a while, West Baden even marketed the stuff as "Pluto Water" so you could enjoy its deleterious effects in the comfort of your own home. "When nature won't, Pluto will." (Historic note: the sale of Pluto Water was halted in 1971, when lithium became a controlled substance.)

The grand hotels were known also, during Prohibition, as places where one could receive "cures" from a staff physician for a variety of maladies and afflictions, such as "melancholy," "nerves" and "seizures." Bacchus, it seems, was a silent partner with Pluto at French Lick.

Today, people do not flock to West Baden either to bathe in, or drink, this odious swill. Instead, they come to marvel at the architecture of its main building and sip wine. At the time of its construction in 1902, it was the largest free-spanning dome world had ever seen. Its beauty and opulence are breathtaking even in our jaded times.

The grand hotels in America became marked for extinction with the 1929 stock market crash and the Great Depression that followed, and the great war that followed that. By the 1950s, as Americans were taking to the Interstate highways to see the Grand Canyon and sleep at a Howard Johnson's, the grand old hotels had faded from the scene, physically and metaphorically. At Howard Johnson's, I recall, the ice cream came in 29 flavors, and the food in one.

The West Baden hotel fell on particularly hard times in the 1930s, when Jesuits converted it into an austere seminary known as West Baden College, stripping away its four Moorish towers. The school limped along for three decades, with little building maintenance to show for it. In 1966, the Jesuits sold it to Macauley and Helen Whiting, who ran a private college there known as the Northwood Institute, until 1983. Larry Bird, the area's most famous native son, briefly took classes at Northwood before moving on to Indiana State University, and then to a brilliant career with the Boston Celtics.

A developer named H. Eugene MacDonald tried briefly to return the property to a hotel, but lacked the resources to do the preservation work

(I sympathize). MacDonald sold the property to another developer in 1985, only to find that the buyer had kited the check to him, and then filed for bankruptcy. This tied up the property in litigation for a decade, during which time Orange County vandals and meth heads smashed what windows remained and looted the property for anything of value.

Even in this decrepit state, my fascination with this building got the better part of me. The sheer incongruity of a massive dome rising out of an empty, hilly Kentuckiana landscape was more than I could resist. In 1992, I hopped the fence and took an unauthorized tour of the place. I was eventually run off by a security guard, who softened a bit when he realized that I was there to gawk at, not loot, the property. Had he been as clueless of my real intentions as most cops today in Kentuckiana, I would most certainly have been facing criminal charges for trespass and maybe a suspension of my law license.

My unauthorized visit in 1992 convinced me that there was no hope for the grand old building, unless a wildly wealthy, idealistic and principled person took the project on as a labor of love. I prayed, fervently, in my *Freidenker* way, for that to happen.

In 1996, my prayers were answered. Bill and Gayle Cook spent $5 million to stabilize the building, with the assistance of Historic Landmarks (f/k/a Historic Landmarks of Indiana, Inc.). In the years that followed, the Cooks eventually completed the restoration not only of the dome but of the sister hotel at French Lick one mile away, at a staggering cost of $100 million.

God, most certainly, is not a Jesuit.

I met Bill and Gayle at the Story Inn shortly before Bill died, and personally thanked them for their efforts to save those buildings. They were the serendipitous guests of John and Carolyn Mutz, John being Indiana's former Lieutenant Governor, and despite of that, both being personal friends. John and Carolyn helped me with another historic project, the Athenaeum, in Indianapolis. It helps to have connections when you're trying to raise $1.5 million for a new roof. We all walked the Story property with wine glasses in hand, and while I talked distractedly about Story's farm-to-table philosophy, my real desire was to learn what motivated these people to make that obviously improvident investment. I relayed to them my story about hopping the fence, and they shared my relief that the statute of limitations had run.

From what I could ascertain, there was nothing motivating the Cooks other than to do the right thing at the right time and their deep love and commitment to preserving Indiana's historic architecture.

Today, these magnificent hotels have been restored to their original opulence, and a fine golf course, replete with foot paths, was constructed to connect them. There's a new 25-meter swimming pool, several restaurants and shops and even game rooms. The old bowling alley still remains. It is a pleasure to sip a glass of wine under the dome at dusk, and enjoy the tasteful indoor light show.

French Lick has a new casino, too, and like every other casino, it is, to me, somewhat sad and seedy. For a time, Donald Trump flirted with the idea of building and operating that casino, but with his casino in Gary having gone bankrupt and owing $18 million to Indiana in back taxes, and his investors once again left holding the bag, "The Donald" either backed away from it or was encouraged to back away from it by Indiana's incisive new governor, Mitch Daniels.

So it could have been a lot worse. A Trump casino in French Lick would have been much seedier than the one they now have. And Trump would almost certainly have taken credit for the resort's turnaround made possible with the Cooks' money, and leveraged that fame into selling a new line of neckties. Or perhaps his hubris would have compelled him to pursue some other outsized ambition.

But the rest of the place is stunning beyond description. The guest rooms are tidy and impeccable. If you ever rent a room at the dome, insist upon one with a window that looks inward. But an outward-facing room is not bad. The gardens, which had become weedy and unkempt from decades of neglect, have been meticulously restored.

French Lick Springs Resort Hotel, of course, is another fine grand hotel. It remained open (barely) even as the Dome was in an advanced state of decay.

French Lick Springs has an interesting history as well. Thomas Taggart, an influential Irish immigrant who served as the mayor of Indianapolis between 1895 and 1901, was a regular customer. When Taggart later became the Chairman of the Democratic National Committee, French Lick Springs Hotel developed a reputation as the unofficial headquarters of the Democratic Party. At Taggart's behest, Franklin Delano Roosevelt secured enough support from party insiders to eventually win his party's nomination for President. This occurred at a Democratic Governor's Conference being held at the hotel in 1931, no doubt in a smoky back room somewhere.

Gambling was the mainstay of French Lick long after the state outlawed it. Then someone discovered, in a way that must have been evocative of Captain Louis Renault's reaction when he learned of gambling at Rick's Café Americain in *Casablanca*, that there was gambling on the premises. In the late 1940s, the casino was shut down.

French Lick Springs also has the distinction of being the first place to serve tomato juice. Tomatoes grow better in Indiana than almost anywhere else on the planet. From late June to mid-September, they are plentiful, and exquisite.

In 1917, Chef Louis Perrin found himself lacking in oranges, and necessity being the mother of invention, he took to squeezing locally-grown tomatoes instead. The rest is history.

If you wish to rest your head in a bed, either resort will do nicely. If you're a first-time visitor, I'd try the Dome first, and then flip a coin after that. The two grand hotels are connected by a streetcar, and if you're so inclined, you can borrow a bike.

For a long time, the rail line that once connected French Lick with the rest of the world dead-ended in a train yard, which became clogged with derelict cars from the 1930s. Orange County meth-heads have little time to spray graffiti, and they have no money to buy spray paint anyway, so these cars remained in relatively pristine condition until the Cooks stepped in.

In the late 1990s, this time accompanied by my younger son Rich, I took another unauthorized tour, this time to see the inside of several vintage train cars. Amazingly, nothing was locked, and there was no security guard to shoo us away. We marveled at the opulence of the cars, and suddenly, it all made sense. It was an easy five-hour sojourn from Chicago to French Lick. In 1902, more train tracks converged in Chicago than any place on earth, bringing famous and infamous people as diverse as Al Capone and Gloria Swanson to French Lick. Husbands wanted to get rid of their wives and kids for a few days, between the end of summer camp and the beginning of school. Hardly anyone owned a car.

As I said, it was a failed business model.

The town of French Lick is, of course, dominated by its two grand hotels. The downtown, or what passes for a downtown, bears the same scars of neglect as its grand hotels. But those scars have healed in amazing way and there are thriving businesses, retail and restaurants.

The excellent French Lick Winery opened its tasting room in the old Beechwood Mansion in 1996. Their new, and much larger, headquarters is located on a bluff that overlooks the town. French Lick Winery has several fine offerings, including one from the Norton grape, grown in Hoosier soil. French Lick is located in the southwest fringe of the Indiana Uplands AVA.

Patoka Lake lies a few miles out of town, a muddy, man-made monstrosity that is the twin of Lake Monroe near Story. South of the LGM, incidentally, there are practically no natural lakes. Humans corrected Mother Nature's mistake by damming up thousands of muddy creeks in Kentuckiana to create new bodies of water, some of them no bigger than a suburban roundabout. In rural areas, these ponds supply drinking and irrigation water, and are stocked with bluegill and bass for some "fee-ish-ing."

On occasion, the government will claim a more extensive area by the power of eminent domain, to create a much larger body of water, usually for the pretext of supplying drinking water to a municipality somewhere, or fostering recreational sports. That's why the town of Elkinsville had to die. All such unnatural bodies of water run thick with silt and farm chemicals, and are destined to become flat bottomlands in a couple of centuries. But until then, we can all enjoy the toxic drinking water and ride around on jet-skis.

Rock quarries dot Kentuckiana, too. They tend to fill up naturally with water, so in order to go about the business of extracting rock or gravel, it is necessary to enlist the help of powerful pumps. When the quarry is retired, it will often turn into a lovely swimming hole. There are several of these near Bloomington, creating an attractive nuisance for venturesome IU students.

Humans have a predilection for clustering around bodies of water. Most of the country's population can be found within a short drive of the ocean or one of the Great Lakes. This human trait has not yet been bred out of Kentuckianans, and real estate developers know it. Thus, you will find numerous condominiums, subdivisions or apartments with a view of a muddy wet basin retention pond or retired rock quarry, oftentimes with names evocative of places on the New England or Gulf coasts. I can understand why a Kentuckiana native, starved for a water view, would want to live near water, but I cannot understand why he would want to live in a place called "Harbour View" or "Misty Cove" and decorate his flat with corals and sea shells.

There are a lot of things I do not understand. For example, why Procter & Gamble in Cincinnati puts tiny polyethylene pellets into Crest toothpaste. Or why parking at the Post Office is limited to 15 minutes, not long enough for you to get to the front of the line.

The largest of these farm ponds, called "lakes," will inevitably sustain a seafood restaurant, incongruously offering saltwater fish, mussels, clams, scallops, shrimp and prawns (most frequently, battered and fried). I've never understood how a lakeside location could confer a competitive advantage upon someone embarking upon the Sisyphean task of making a wholesome meal out of Chilean farm-raised salmon, but I will confess again, there are a great many things in this world that I do not understand. For example, I do not understand why Catholics don't think that fish is meat, or why we still need to be punished after God forgives us at Confession.

Such Kentuckiana eateries are always decorated with piers, planks, buoys, life rings and mooring ropes, and inevitably a marlin trophy in the tavern, to give the impression that you're on the Gulf coast of Alabama and the shrimp boat just pulled in. It is an eerie sight to behold, but the customers don't seem to be bothered by the discordance.

Orange, and surrounding counties, are nearly as white, and sparsely populated, as Brown County. The same two ethnic groups, Germans and Scotch-Irish, predominate. However, the German settlers were of a different stock than you will find in Indianapolis, Cincinnati, Milwaukee, and other such places. Here are large communities of Amish, attempting, as best they can, to scratch a living from the soil while eschewing the benefits and curses of modern technology.

The Amish were Anabaptists who migrated from Switzerland and southern Germany beginning in the 18th century. Though estimates of their population vary, it is likely that there are now more than 200,000 of them in the United States, and about 20% of those make their home in Indiana. To varying degrees, they all refuse to adopt technology (though I have seen some of them driving cars). They have retained high pre-industrial birth rates, while embracing modern medicine to a sufficient extent to reduce infant mortality to post-industrial levels. As a result, they are following Christ's edict to be fruitful and multiply.

The Amish are pacifists. Back before Richard Nixon ended the draft in 1974, allowing me to legally avoid a taxpayer-funded trip to Vietnam, the Amish were exempt from military service. I have never had the occasion to pick a fight with one, so I cannot be certain how they might react when provoked. If Amish teenagers wore Nikes, I'd step on one just to see the reaction.

Except during the "Rumspringa," when Amish parents wisely kick their teenagers out of the house until they regain their mental faculties, drug use among these people is very low. Needless to say, the crime rate in Amish country is very low too.

At the Story Inn, we serve maple syrup from local Amish farmers, and for a while, I personally made the trek to Orleans, Indiana, to fetch it from Ervin Bontrager. Ervin's farm is typical of Amish homesteads: no phone, no electricity, no running water, no mechanical farm equipment. But the place is immaculate. I once used his outdoor privy in mid-summer, and it was far cleaner than the men's restroom at the "Flying J" Truck Stop in Greenwood.

The place was notably free of flies and mosquitoes, despite the lack of pesticides. That's because the family had enticed a large colony of purple martins to settle there. Purple martins nest in apartment-like colonies and dine voraciously on bugs. Ervin didn't know it, but he could have been certified as an USDA organic farmer. (Not long ago, "organic" simply meant the presence of a carbon atom; the federal government has literally appropriated that word from the English language, by means of a previously unrecognized linguistic power of eminent domain.)

Ervin takes his horse-drawn cart to the forest near his home and collects buckets of sap, which he then boils down into syrup (95% escapes as steam) in a wood-fired sugar shack right next to his home. His evaporator, oddly enough, is stainless steel. The syrup is the most coveted light-amber in color, and it is the best I have ever tasted.

When we need some syrup, I must write Ervin an old-fashioned letter. I always get a reply within a week. Ervin accepts cash, period. His prices are very reasonable, especially if you buy in bulk. Once I bought a 55-gallon drum of the stuff for just over $2,000. After we shook on it, he issued an ear-piercing whistle, and three friendly kids in straw hats showed up and loaded the drum onto the back of my pick-up truck (they had a ramp handy—no forklift needed). Ervin didn't want the drum back, but when I buy syrup in glass jugs from him, he expects me to return them.

Ervin's wife and delightful daughters sell homemade pies and cinnamon buns as well. On a recent visit, Jane and I bought more than a few samples, not many of which survived the trek back to Story. Jane was able to photograph the Bontragers' kitchen, which contained only a wood-burning stove. The Amish do not like to be photographed themselves, for reasons which make perfect, practical sense to me in this age of technological intrusion and government surveillance. To my knowledge, the government has yet to mandate a "black box" to be installed in Amish buggies, 2014 and newer.

Most Amish speak German at home, and Ervin is no exception. I speak the standard modern dialect of German, *Hochdeutsch*. I find the *Amish-Sprache* to be almost unintelligible. That doesn't matter. There's not much else to discuss with Ervin, since he knows almost nothing of life in Germany, or for that matter, life outside of Orange County. The Amish typically drop out of school after the eighth grade.

The trip from Brown to Orange County is not without its points of interest, particularly if you are willing to go underground. Northern Kentuckiana is dominated by Karst topography. Eons ago, most of the area was a shallow tropical sea, and as countless carbonate-bearing organisms died and settled to the bottom, a considerable amount of limestone was formed. In Bloomington, Bedford, Mitchell and other places, this limestone is still quarried for building materials. The Empire State Building in New York City is faced with Indiana limestone.

Limestone is alkaline, and rain water is slightly acidic. When the two come into contact, the chemical reaction between them inevitably leads to erosion and highly mineralized water that wreaks havoc with water heaters and metal pipes. Over millennia, Northern Kentuckiana has become honeycombed with some of the world's most extensive caves and underground rivers.

One of those is Bluespring Caverns near Bedford, which contains 21 miles of surveyed passages and the longest subterranean river in the United States. Three miles of that river is actually navigable. Jane and I took an electric boat ride a couple of years ago, a jaw-dropping experience. At this point, the river runs quiet and deep. The guide took us past spectacular mineral formations which were shiny, sometimes glittering, and always colorful. And then, at what seemed to be the most distant point, the driver shut off the flood light and engine, so that we could experience a moment of complete sensory deprivation. It was a total lack of light, and sound, that one cannot experience on the surface. He then slapped two seat cushions together, creating a report that sounded like gunfire and seemed to echo for minutes.

More recently, Jane and I explored two caves near Corydon, Squire Boone Caverns and Indiana Caverns.

As the name implies, Squire Boone was discovered by Squire Boone. Squire was the brother of Daniel Boone, a veteran of the Revolutionary War, and one of Kentuckiana's earliest pioneers. Pioneering was dangerous work. And while Daniel is the hero who got his own TV series and a generation of kids singing his praises, it was Squire who searched Kentuckiana for Daniel and saved his life. Indeed, this was such a hostile place that of the eight white men who first explored Kentuckiana, only two came out—and Daniel made it only because of his brother.

Squire stumbled upon the cave in 1790, when taking refuge to escape a band of Native Americans who probably suspected that the newcomers were going to steal their land. He later returned to the area with his family, opened a grist mill, and had an almost mystical attachment to the cave. His remains were laid to rest in that cave, in accordance with his wishes, and so they remain (albeit in a new coffin, the other having long ago fallen apart).

The Squire Boone cave has prodigious mineral formations, indicating that it is quite old. Like most Kentuckiana caves, a river flows through this one, rushing more than a million gallons of water through the numerous waterfalls, but you must take the tour on foot.

Indiana Caverns is the newest Kentuckiana cave to be opened to the public. The cave's natural entrance was too small for a corpulent tourist to squeeze through it, so Nature's mistake was corrected with the help of some dynamite. The tour, which takes about 90 minutes, is mostly on foot, but there's a short ride by electric boat that will take you to the furthest accessible point. (The "river," which continues for miles beyond that point, is so shallow that it actually had to be dammed to accommodate our pontoon boat.) Indiana Caverns has a notable dearth of stalactites and stalagmites, but contains a treasure trove of Ice Age bones, including bison and bear. No human remains have been discovered, yet.

There are two more memorable caves nearby, Wyandotte which just recently re-opened, and Marengo, which was discovered only in 1883. The later has been open to the public for some time. I remember seeing billboards for it when I was an undergraduate at IU, eons ago, about the time the earth's crust had solidified.

These caves, which extend for dozens of miles each, have not been fully explored even today. If you desire to become the first person to set foot in one of them, you might not wish to do so if there is a threat of rain. Water punches through sink-holes and other points of access and can create immediate flooding underground. The temperature of caves is a constant 54 degrees Fahrenheit, and with the exception of the occasional flood underground, caves are timeless. They smell, and feel, like a dank basement wine cellar.

Because these caves extend for dozens of miles, one might think they might be linked in some fashion. Oddly enough, they are not. This profound isolation creates brand new ecosystems, and additional confirmation of Darwin's theory of evolution, which many surface dwellers in Kentuckiana continue to deny. The tour of Indiana Caverns is preceded by a short video which dances around this inconvenient truth.

Occasionally, some poor creature from the surface, like a crawdad or salamander, gets sucked into one of these caves and manages to survive on detritus that drops in from the surface. If it can find a mate in the darkness, the process of speciation kicks into high gear, and the cave-dwellers quickly lose eyes and pigment, and develop massive antennae. There's a lot of bacteria in caves, but no plants, for obvious reasons.

Some of these caves are home to bats, which have evolved an exquisite means of getting around by echolocation. Unfortunately, Kentuckiana's bat population is under siege. There's a fungus afoot, always fatal to a bat which becomes infected with it. Since bats do us community service by munching on mosquitoes, we humans will need to invest in more DEET, particularly as the Zika virus makes its way north. (Kentuckiana lies at the northern range of the *Aedes aegypti* mosquito, which carries Zika.)

On the surface, life is less interesting. Bedford has a Wal-Mart and a McDonalds (though as Jane points out, it also has a Starbucks, which in her Progressive mind is a sure sign of civilization). Mitchell has even less to offer. Jane and I desperately wanted to buy a nice bottle of wine in Mitchell, but the pickings were so slim that we decided to skip alcohol for an entire day. Notably, Mitchell is the childhood home of astronauts Virgil I. ("Gus") Grissom, Charles D. Walker and Kenneth D. Bowersox. They were all determined, apparently, to get as far away from Mitchell as possible.

Spring Mill State Park is a lovely park near Mitchell that is worth visiting. In comparison to the Brown County State Park, it is diminutive—a mere 1,600 acres. But it's got its own caves, too, and even a reconstructed 1816 settler village replete with a functioning watermill. The village was a major stagecoach stop for those going from east to west. Colonel Richard H. Lieber may be credited for spearheading the creating of this park, as well as the restoration of its village. Bring wine.

Indiana has 92 counties, too many to have efficient governmental administration. Efforts to consolidate some of the lesser-populated counties has been met with opposition, for the usual turf-battle reasons. In Kentuckiana, a least, the county courthouse serves as the centerpiece of each county seat, a quaint anachronism known as the "courthouse square." All of Kentuckiana's county seat towns are laid out in this fashion, and it's a visual treat of real small-town Americana.

If you travel Kentuckiana by any route other than the Interstate, you'll see several small towns centered around a tidy, and remarkably ornate, courthouses. These towns obviously desired to define themselves by the beauty of their courthouses, and with very few exceptions, they survive intact. Just don't find yourself confined to the inside of one of them on a Saturday night after tippling one too many in a local tavern. These towns are starved for revenue, and an out-of-town license plate is itself probable cause to pull you over.

Time for a rant.

Our lovely legislators have fortified the constabulary's already considerable powers with civil forfeiture laws. Ostensibly designed to deprive crooks of ill-gotten gains, these laws incentivize cops to seize your property upon the flimsiest suspicion of criminal activity, since they allow local police departments to keep most, if not all, of the property seized.

Having too much cash in your possession is one such pretext. They'll confiscate it from you, and require you to prove, by a preponderance of evidence in a local courtroom kindly disposed to such local cops, that the property was not ill-gotten and that you deserve to have it back. Incredibly, cops will now sometimes seize your property without even charging you with a crime. That shifts possession to the cops and the burden of proof to you to get it back (as they say, possession is nine-tenths of the law). So much for "due process" and the presumption of innocence until proven guilty.

Cops will sometimes knowingly let a "buzzed" suspect go after confiscating his cash, secure in the knowledge that they'll never see the suspect again.

One would expect such shenanigans from cops in Tijuana or Juarez, but in fact, our beloved boys in blue and brown have become some of the best shakedown artists on the planet, with local prosecutors sometimes in on the action. (Prosecutors will sometimes agree to "drop" the charges if you agree to forfeit the cash. If you're facing an increase in insurance rates, that one's a no-brainer.)

It may be tempting just to hand the cash over to the cop who detains you, and then politely ask if you may leave. Though seldom enforced, bribery of a cop is still a crime on the books here, so this must be done with great subtlety. Once I was detained by a cop in Chihuahua, Mexico, on my way to a business meeting. I put several 20s into the trunk of the car, and the cop graciously let me continue my journey. You can't be that brazen in most parts of Kentuckiana.

For this reason, I advise my clients never to carry more than a grand in cash. In rural America, cops are more dangerous than crooks. Suck it out of an ATM only as you need it.

But cash has one undeniable benefit: it is largely untraceable. For that reason, I advise my clients to always pay for alcohol with cash, never a credit card. Credit card purchases leave a trail, making you easy prey for local law enforcement. If you're enjoying dinner in a restaurant, ask your server split the tab between food and alcohol, and pay for the latter with cash.

And for Bacchus's sake, if a cop shines a light in your face and asks if you've been drinking, ALWAYS say no. Just lie. There's no down side to lying to a cop who's looking for any pretext to shake you down for money. It's a Clinton thing that just might save your career as a crooked lawyer, politician, philanthropist or hedge fund manager.

End of rant.

Your drive to French Lick could take you through the town of Paoli, the seat of Orange County. There you will find a tidy white courthouse faced on all sides by little shops, a flashback to the early 20th century. Mercifully, they built the Wal-Mart a couple of miles to the north, leaving the old town in pristine condition. The land is hilly this far south of the LGM, creating a good topography for skiing. Unfortunately, it hardly ever snows in Paoli. There is, in fact, a ski lodge called "Paoli Peaks" built by stoic Swiss immigrants who didn't have the good sense to know when to quit. I blame it on the weather. Jane blames it on climate change caused by recalcitrant Republicans driving SUVs with stick families pasted on the back window.

To the south and west of Orange County, not far from Evansville, is a cultural and architectural oddity, New Harmony. Once again, German immigrants made their impression. Like the Anabaptists, the Harmonists were escaping religious persecution in Europe. Unlike the Anabaptists, the Harmonists believed that you could be fruitful without multiplying. The Harmonists are all gone, possibly because they practiced celibacy.

In 1814, Johann Georg Rapp acquired 20,000 acres of Indiana wilderness near the Wabash River for $2/acre, not a trivial sum in that day, and led his followers, the Harmonists, to create a prosperous little settlement. One wonders what compelled them to work so hard, since the Harmonists believed that Christ would return in their lifetime and he was not keen on his followers taking grain, tools and furniture with them upon their ascension into heaven.

Among all of humanity's sexual deviations, celibacy is perhaps the most peculiar. We humans have co-opted sex for more than reproduction. Sex cements pair-bonds, which keep families intact so that we can raise brainy children who spend 15 years reaching sexual maturity, and yet another 15 years reaching intellectual maturity. A well-adjusted child needs to have highly romantically involved parents. Sometimes, it helps if they are married to each other, but that is optional.

For reasons which elude me many, or most, religions criminalize, or at least attempt to regulate, sexual practices. This seems as futile as attempting to regulate the time the sun will rise, or the change of the seasons. The vow of celibacy taken by Catholic priests not only serves no function, it is unnatural. In its worst manifestations, children often become the object of suppressed priestly sexual desire.

Likewise, the Catholic prohibition against artificial birth control runs against the grain of human nature. The desire to use "artificial" birth control is natural when you can expect all of your offspring to survive and be healthy. The infant mortality rate is lower now than it's been in all of human history, and I would submit to you that this is a very good thing. People voluntarily limit family size once they're convinced that all their kids will survive to adulthood. Furthermore, fewer births enables families to afford an SUV to haul those kids to soccer practice.

It is among history's bitterest ironies that it was the celibate Pope Paul VI who made that pronouncement in *Humanae vitae*, in 1968. Not surprisingly, the Church's prohibition against artificial birth control is widely ignored by Catholics of breeding age, and Catholics do not produce children in any greater numbers than Methodists, Presbyterians or even Pentecostals.

It was about that time that Paul Ehrlich from Stanford wrote the *Population Bomb*, predicting a Malthusian disaster for our species. No small portion of his vitriol was directed at the papal prohibition against artificial birth control, since Catholicism is the world's largest religious group, today representing about half of the world's Christians, and 17% of total human population. (Ehrlich, incidentally, had himself sterilized so that he would not contribute to the problem.)

I read this book with great interest and consternation. Fortunately, Ehrlich's as well as Malthus's concerns proved to be mostly unfounded. Demographic transition from high birth and death rates to low birth and death rates has occurred in the majority of countries, and did so much faster than even the most optimistic demographers would have predicted at that time. As a species, we're nearly at the magical "Total Fertility Rate" of 2.1 births per female, which is replacement level. Birth rates have dropped dramatically in east and south Asia, and Europe's birth rate has been below replacement level for several decades, forcing governments to plan for turning the whole continent into the world's largest nursing home. Clearly, very few people heeded Pope Paul VI's edict.

The precipitous fall in birth rates is both a cause and an effect of longer life expectancies, better nutrition, higher literacy, and, of course, greater wealth. Periodically, I am asked to teach a course in International Law at Butler University. I begin the semester by asking students what future historians will find most significant about the period 1950-present. Inevitably, I get the "First black president" and "Marriage equality," answers you would expect from kids whose minds have been filled with mush. The more incisive ones will say "Invention of the Internet." No one has yet mentioned: The vast creation of wealth.

Two countries alone, China and India, comprising a bit more than a third of the human race, have created more wealth than all of humanity did before 1950. Deng Xiaoping famously said, "It doesn't matter if the cat is black or white, as long as it catches mice." His pragmatic economic reforms made possible China's stunning success, and fueled the unprecedented explosion of international trade in goods, services and ideas. Deng's got my vote as the greatest figure of the 20th century.

Conservatives maligned China's "one child" policy, and it is obligatory for every US president to berate China about its "human rights" record. This is in keeping with America's role as the world's leading exporter of moral rectitude. China's "one child" policy, now largely abandoned, probably prevented 300,000,000 births. At the conclusion of one of those lectures, Deng reportedly asked Ronald Reagan, "So how many millions are you willing to take"?

When I was a child, half of the human race lived in abject poverty (earning less than $2/day). Today, less than 15% of the human race lives under such conditions, and that is falling very rapidly. I might actually live long enough to see this kind of poverty eliminated completely. (Income inequality is a problem to be addressed another day.)

Five decades ago, demographers were predicting that human population would peak at around 15 billion, at which point Malthus would begin taking his grim toll. Countries have transitioned from high birth/death rates to low birth/death rates faster than anyone back then would have optimistically predicted, causing demographers to revise that number downward. (Mexico's birth rate has dropped by two-thirds since 1960, bringing it in line with ours. It looks like we won't need to build that wall after all.) The smart money now predicts that human population will peak at about nine billion, and that no one will starve. I would submit to you that these are very good things.

It remains to be seen whether this vast creation of wealth will also inaugurate an era of peace. I came of age at a time when B-52s were constantly aloft, bristling with nuclear weapons, poised to strike at the Soviet Union. My father actually built a bomb shelter in the basement, assuming we would survive a blast when the Soviets took out Pittsburgh. No matter how prickly the Chinese might get about a couple of worthless islets in the South China Sea, I remain cautiously optimistic that we'll see the wisdom not to take out Apple's iPhone plant in Chengdu.

Homosexuality, likewise, is frowned upon by Catholics and many other religious groups. Homosexuals comprise a constant three or so percent of human population, no matter how much discrimination they must endure. One would initially be persuaded that any activity which is not conducive to gene propagation would ultimately be selected out of the human genome. But E.O. Wilson notes that this trait is so prevalent, and ubiquitous, that it cannot be explained as a genetic mutation, and his insight on this point is prescient.

Wilson argues that homosexuality is the product of group, not individual, selection, the same process that selects humans for altruistic behavior. Gays contribute disproportionately to art, music, science, literature and a host of things that enrich the lives of us all, and those contributions to society more than outweigh their own lack of children, genetically speaking. Maybe it's time the religious freaks let up on the gays.

The Harmonists' experiment was short-lived, and the community decided to sell and return *en masse* to Pennsylvania. Robert Owen, a Welsh industrialist and idealistic kook, bought the town of Harmony in 1825 and set out to create a utopian community. He re-named it "New Harmony," the name that sticks today. Owen did not restrict sex and instead focused on educating the common man by opening libraries well before Andrew Carnegie did.

The Owenite social experiment was a failure, for all of the usual reasons that utopian societies fail. Anyone ever hear of the "tragedy of the commons"? Nobel Laureate Elinor Ostrom from Indiana University had an interesting take on this concept, one too nuanced to relate here.

Today, New Harmony is a tidy little community of about 800 residents, with many of the old architectural treasures intact. There are some quaint shops along its main street, and people get around on bicycles or golf carts when the weather is nice. It's worth a visit just to gawk at the buildings, read historic placards, and to walk its tree-lined boulevards.

To the east of New Harmony are multiple villages and towns settled mostly by German Catholics. These are my people.

Jasper is still so infested with people of German Catholic descent that its residents all share a compulsion to clean up trash, wash windows, and mow grass so short that the lawns look like putting greens. Otherwise, they'll feel guilty. German frugality and enterprise are everywhere in evidence. People here marry once, work hard, save much, spend little, live long, and die with impressive estates that become easy prey for the tax man.

Everyone in Jasper owns a Dachshund named "Fritz." There's a community bank there called the "German-American Bank." All of the people in Jasper, not just the children, are above average.

There's a German comedy club in Jasper, too, I'm told. The jokes are not funny, but the show always starts on time.

The German Catholic immigrants to the area quickly set out to recreate some of the old monasteries and cathedrals of Europe. Jasper has some stunning churches. But the mother of all churches, if you will pardon the expression, is the Monastery of the Immaculate Conception in nearby Ferdinand, circa 1867.

This magnificent building is the ecclesiastical equivalent to the West Baden Springs Hotel (offering Holy Water instead of Pluto Water, but cures nevertheless). It is evocative of the great cathedral of Munich, where I once attended Mass only for the purpose of deceiving my father that I had not become a *Freidenker*. (I took communion—may God strike me dead.) Today, Immaculate Conception houses one of the largest communities of Benedictine nuns in the United States.

Like most notable Catholic enterprises, there is a gift shop nearby, offering religious and secular memorabilia. (The Church's practice of selling indulgences has long been abandoned, but marriage nullifications are still for sale, and quite dear. I am in need of three.) Jane and I were there at Christmas time, and I was happy to find some familiar German *Kekse*, baked in the Old World style by the nuns. The sisters who run the Monastery are very good marketers and mail their cookies worldwide, and are now listed as "Indiana Artisans."

Ferdinand is badly in need of a rathskeller.

CHAPTER 15. THE SOUTH

> Mammy: "Oh now, Miss Scarlett, you
> come on and eat jess a little, honey!"
>
> Scarlet: "No! I'm going to have a good time
> today, and do my eating at the barbeque."
>
> —Gone with the Wind (1939)

When you cross the Ohio River into Louisville, you also cross the so-called "Mason–Dixon Line." Sort of.

The Mason–Dixon line was surveyed by Charles Mason and Jeremiah Dixon between 1763 and 1767 to settle a boundary dispute between Pennsylvania, Maryland and Delaware. That's a long way from Kentuckiana. Their Iroquois guides refused to take them any further than Mt. Morris in Pennsylvania, for fear of intruding upon the lands of the Lenape. Thus, the originally surveyed line did not go this far west.

The line was extended in the years that followed, giving unearned credit to Mason (an astronomer) and Dixon (a surveyor), and that line eventually came to symbolize the cultural boundary between the American North and the South. The Ohio River obviously served as a convenient, albeit inaccurate, point at which to lay a cultural and political boundary.

Nevertheless, the fact that you enter "Dixie" by crossing over into Louisville conjures the image of a Yankee army amassing in Jeffersonville to strike at the heart of Louisville and burn it to the ground, and gallant Southern gentlemen on horseback hastily gathering to defend it to the last man, while fainting Southern ladies are being herded by their faithful Negro house servants to the relative safety of a plantation somewhere.

In point of fact, though Kentucky was a slave state, it never entered the Civil War.

The Ohio River was a superhighway which brought new people and helped to create a unique culture. It did not divide people and cultures. As a point of cultural demarcation, the LGM would have worked much better. Mason and Dixon, for all their learning and travels, didn't know about the glacier.

Louisville is but the largest of several Kentuckiana river towns. These towns took root on both sides of the great Ohio, and the ones on the north side of the river don't look a whole lot different from the ones on the south side of the river. One of them, Corydon, briefly served as Indiana's state capital.

I'll digress for a moment. Corydon is not actually a river town, but it is close. It's a charming village of about 3,000 souls, which served as the capital of the Indiana territory, and later state, from 1813 to 1825. The capital building, now a museum, is as small as a pretentious suburban home. The Story Inn's General Store building is actually larger. One gets a perspective of Indiana's early days by touring it. Ironically, Corydon, the former capital of a "northern" state, is located about 25 miles due west of Louisville, situated in a "southern" state. Thank the Ohio River's winding path for that.

Ergo, Louisville is not a cultural gateway to the South, with the "South" reaching its cultural apex in Savannah or Charleston hundreds of miles on, where people suddenly become polite and say things like "bless your heart" and invite you onto their porch for some sweet iced tea. Rather, Louisville is the heart and soul of Kentuckiana, a place that has its own culture and ought to be a state in its own right. It is the center of horse racing and bourbon-making. Its fine universities possess excellent basketball teams, so the place doesn't seem to suffer for the lack of a professional franchise. Indiana University, University of Louisville, and the University of Kentucky (in nearby Lexington) have a three-way rivalry so full of vitriol that it could only arise between blood brothers.

Any visitor to Louisville should, as a courtesy, first learn how to pronounce its name correctly. Kentuckiana natives habitually add syllables to words. Louisville natives actually remove a syllable, in this one instance. Flatlanders see a three-syllable word, pronounced "Loo-eee-ville." Natives collapse it into two syllables: "Looil-vul." The first syllable requires a glottal sound that, if done incorrectly, could easily telophase into a second syllable. It is imperative that you practice saying "Looil-vul" in front of a mirror before attempting to employ it in conversation. If you fail, you will sound stupider than Joe Biden mimicking black English in an Atlanta church. Kentuckianans north of the Ohio River know how to pronounce "Louisville" correctly.

People in Indiana/Kentuckiana have a long history of butchering the pronunciation of place names they have borrowed from somewhere else.

There are two towns above the LGM, spelled "Chile" and "Peru," which are pronounced "Cheye-lie" and "Pee-roo." There's a county spelled "Pulaski" but pronounced "Polas-cow." Below the LGM, there's a town spelled "Versailles" and a county spelled "Dubois," and these are respectively pronounced "Versayles" and "Doo-boys." Just 10 miles south of Story is a tiny town spelled "Houston" but pronounced "House-tun." One does not challenge the way one pronounces the name of the place where he sleeps, so as a courtesy, visitors must adopt the vernacular in every instance.

In Kentuckiana, by the way, people who retire to the bedroom "suite" pronounce it "suit."

When Jane and I visit Louisville, we are always impressed with its fine restaurants (Louisville has the most independent restaurants for a city its size in the U.S.) and hotels, cool shops and art studios along its old tobacco (now Hipster) warehouse district. We could spend a hundred pages describing its stately historic neighborhoods and its urban-bourbon attractions. I will yield to my own geek fascination only by describing, with brevity, its two grand hotels, the Seelbach and the Brown.

The Seelbach was established by two brothers from Bavaria, Lewis and Otto Seelbach, with the goal of recreating the opulence of Europe's grand hotels. The structure incorporated marble from Germany, Italy and France, and wood from the West Indies and Europe. More than 25,000 people were on hand to celebrate its grand opening on May 1, 1905. With 500 rooms, restaurants, bars and a rooftop garden, the Seelbach was easily Louisville's largest, and most opulent, hotel. In the years that followed, the Seelbach became the favorite grazing spot and watering hole for the top brass of Louisville's signature event, the Kentucky Derby. (The Seelbach bar, just off the lobby, offers at least 100 different bourbons, costing as much as $225 per shot. Too rich for my blood.)

Louis and Otto had the good sense to sell out before the 1929 stock market crash, making them unique among grand hotel visionaries by not facing the indignity of going broke. Successive owners made a decent go of it, though the place fell on hard times in the 1970s. The Grand Dame stood vacant for several years while the rest of the country was suffering through Watergate and its aftermath. But then Roger Davis, Bill Cook's Doppelganger, restored and re-opened it in 1982.

I stayed in the Seelbach for the first time in 1983 and was rendered speechless by its lobby and winding staircases. I make it a point to return every few years. The basement has Kentuckiana's most ornate *rathskeller*, which is not surprising, considering brothers Louis and Otto's ambitions and German ancestry. Really important decisions take place in *rathskellers*, or at least they used to be. If there were more *rathskellers*, there would be fewer wars.

Today, the Seelbach is managed by Hilton, and despite the international branding and Hilton-uniformed staff, the place retains its original charm and elegance. Lots of potted palms. Ditch the wines and have a bourbon.

Just a few blocks away from the Seelbach is the Brown Hotel, built on a grand scale in 1923 by James Graham Brown. The Brown is similar in size and accouterments to the Seelbach, but oddly, its lobby is one flight up from street level, depriving visitors of that all-important "wow" first impression. Like the Seelbach, the Brown catered to the local and visiting bluebloods.

Like all of America's grand hotels of this era, the Great Depression hit the Brown hard. James Graham Brown defaulted on his loan, and the bank threatened foreclosure. To keep the place open, Brown asked his employees to serve without pay. Many did, enabling the Brown to keep its doors open.

In 1926, hotel Chef Fred K. Schmidt introduced the "Hot Brown," an open-faced turkey sandwich with bacon, ladled with a Mornay sauce with, occasionally, a dash of paprika on top for color and zest. Local legend has it that the chef created this treat as comfort food for Louisville's working ladies, who were seeking sustenance after a hard night's labors in the wee hours between Speakeasy closure and sunrise church service. Today, the "Hot Brown" is nearly as famous as the hotel in which it was born.

In 1937, Louisville was hit by a terrible flood that inundated the Brown's first floor. One worker is recorded as having caught a two-pound fish in the Brown's lower lobby. The hotel remained open, without electrical service, to serve as housing for Louisville's displaced residents.

A $1.5 million renovation in 1965 could not stem the effects of the city's decline in the 1960s and 1970s, and business at the Brown suffered. James Graham Brown died in 1969, and the hotel closed its doors two years later. The building was sold to the Louisville Public Schools, and for about a decade served as the headquarters for the city's troubled school system. Its toll on the building was predictable. A civic group known as the "Broadway Group" then acquired the building, and began its renovation in 1983. It was an eerie parallel with the second coming of the Seelbach. Today, the Brown has been restored to its former glamour.

The best view of Louisville, incidentally, is from the north bank of the Ohio, at the Falls of the Ohio State Park. There you can see the city's skyline with the mighty Ohio in the foreground. At that point, the river is traversed by an old iron railroad bridge that speaks unmistakably of America's early industrial period. This place is significant for two reasons. It holds a treasure trove of fossils that have been exposed by the shifting waters of the Ohio, and it is the place where Lewis and Clark met to begin their expedition west to a place that would eventually be called Oregon. In 1992, Indiana built a large interpretative center and museum, well worth the visit.

The Kentuckiana that surrounds Louisville is a beautiful land of rolling hills, horse farms, quaint towns and, of course, distilleries. The place does have its warts, too.

Now I will rant.

My candidate for the most benighted place in Kentuckiana sits just 40 miles north of Louisville: Austin, Indiana. Austin stands company with various decrepit towns like Scottsburg, Brownstown and Sellersburg, a region fast becoming known as the "Republic of Opana."

Austin is a place worth visiting just once in a lifetime, only for the purpose of observing first-hand the cumulative effects that meth, oxymorphine and heroin can have on a shrinking population of addicts possessed of sub-normal IQs. The HIV infection rate in Austin is comparable to what you would find in the red light district of Lagos. In fact, the HIV problem in Austin is so bad that Indiana's former governor, Mike Pence, approved a needle exchange program in an attempt to stem the rate of infection. (Sadly, Pence's moment of lucidity was short-lived; thereafter, he accepted Donald Trump's invitation to be his running mate.)

If human vision could pierce aluminum and vinyl, enabling one to observe a typical Austin family's charming scene of domesticity these days, one would witness needle-sharing among three generations gathered around a Formica dining room table. This is not a picture-postcard view of white rural America.

Kentuckiana's drug problem, of course, is not confined to Austin's town limits. Meth and heroin are claiming the lives of young people everywhere, at an alarming rate. These drugs disproportionately affect the poorer, less educated population. Maybe it's Darwin at work. Maybe this is another explanation for the "Flynn Effect."

More than eighty people die from drug overdose in the United States each day, which is comparable to the number of people who die in traffic accidents. (The actual death rate from overdose is probably much higher, since the cause of death is frequently misreported as heart attacks or strokes by local coroners who are loth to expose the sordid details of deaths in their communities because they must stand for election.) This happens despite the fact that cops and paramedics are now equipped with naloxone, a truly remarkable drug that counteracts heroin. Thus, more overdose victims than ever are surviving to shoot up another day. Progress.

Heroin is about as cheap as beer, thanks to our improvident meddling in foreign lands where poppies are a cash crop. If I were an Islamist militant dedicated to America's destruction, I'd let up on the suicide bombings and beheading of priests for a while and focus on ways to make heroin even cheaper.

It goes without saying that our police, prosecutors, schools and political leaders have proved themselves unfit to meet this challenge. The so-called "war on drugs" has landed two million Americans in jails and prisons, yet drugs are cheaper, and more plentiful, than ever. The meth and heroin addicts who become incarcerated are actually the lucky ones. They're less likely to die than the ones who don't get caught.

In Brown County, I've seen good citizens report meth lab activity to a member of the local idiot police, only to be stonewalled. Houses and trailers burn down to the ground with alarming frequency, with few consequences. In 2015, hunters stumbled upon an acre of carefully tended cannabis just one mile from Story. No arrests. The local police blamed it on Mexicans.

I can't make this up. I guess we need to build a wall.

End of rant.

A road trip to the Kentuckiana that lies to south of Louisville is not complete without a visit to one of its famous distilleries. A couple of years ago, Jane and I took a lovely tour of the Buffalo Trace Distillery near Frankfort. We traveled there by bus from Louisville as guests of the local Convention and Visitor's Bureau, along with a gaggle of travel writers. No doubt these transportation arrangements were made with our own safety in mind.

Fermentation is the action of yeast upon sugar. Yeast can consume many different kinds of sugars—sucrose, fructose, glucose, etc.— whether they occur in grapes, grain, exotic fruits, potatoes, dandelions or old tires. The by-product of fermentation, alcohol (ethanol), is much coveted by humans and other animals. But to the yeast that produces it, alcohol is a waste product.

Carbon dioxide is another waste product. The presence of both waste products in sparkling wine sounds better when labeled *méthode champaignoise*.

During fermentation, the alcohol reaches toxic concentrations, killing the yeast. The fermentation process ceases naturally when alcohol reaches 17 or 18 percent, which causes the yeast to suffocate. The boldest "hot" Australian shirazes reach this level. Most American wines are lower in alcohol. Beer, which has much less alcohol than wine, can actually contain live yeast cultures, which add to flavor and assist in digestion.

Newsflash: Microbes are overwhelmingly beneficial, or harmless, to humans. That's good, because within our own bodies, "foreign" bacteria outnumber our own cells by ten to one. We wouldn't be able to digest our food without them.

In order to concentrate alcohol above 17 or 18 percent, it must go through the distillation process, which simply involves boiling and condensing it. This is possible because alcohol is volatile and has a lower boiling point than water.

Whiskey, of course, requires distillation. At Buffalo Trace, Jane and I saw fermentation and distillation on an industrial scale. But the distilled product is unpalatable without the additional step of barreling and aging.

We saw that in a magnificent timber warehouse at the distillery. Thousands of barrels of whiskey in slots all supported by old-growth timbers, lagged together. This old warehouse was supporting the weight of a packed parking garage. Very impressive.

When whiskey ages in an oak barrel, some of it escapes as vapor. Distillers call the missing part the "angel's share." As I walked the hallways of this monument to yeast and human ingenuity, I was struck by the most pleasant, sweet aroma; it was an olfactory blessing from a host of seraphim.

Our tour guide cautioned us to extinguish any tobacco, which is wise counsel since alcohol is highly flammable. A Toyota Prius could actually burn it for fuel, if necessary. But that would be a sin against Bacchus and his many angels. If the Buffalo Trace warehouse ever caught fire, it would burn like a refinery. Come to think of it, Buffalo Trace *is* a refinery.

For me, tasting whiskey is actually less pleasant than smelling it. I can actually appreciate a cigar, too, but only as a second-hand smoker.

Wine tasting and whiskey tasting requires very different software. Wine tasting is a ritual that begins with the pouring of one or two ounces into a wide-mouthed glass, spinning it to release the aromatics, sniffing it in deliberate bursts, and, finally, after a minute or two, tasting it, with audible slurps, before swallowing. The process is not complete until you slowly exhale through your nose, to absorb the wine's "finish," while your tongue explores the roof of your mouth for lingering tannins.

If you attempt to taste whiskey in this manner, you will singe your nose hairs and probably incur a bit of brain damage as well. A little bit of whiskey goes a long way. Like wine, whiskey can be subtle, as long as you turn down the volume. No one wants to hear his favorite tune at 160 decibels.

Whiskey, of course, is frequently blended with cola, juices, tonics and other dreadful things to create an alcoholic abomination known as the "mixed drink." Louisvillians are particularly fond of one called the "Mint Julep," which genteel ladies wearing sun hats slurp at the race track while they gossip about their infidelities.

Kentuckiana south of the Ohio is the only place you can find true "bourbon," which is simply whiskey made primarily by fermenting corn.

Corn, or maize, itself has an interesting history, worth at least a hundred pages of geek-prattle. I'll be succinct.

Corn is native to the Americas, and probably achieved the improbable shape of its ear as a result of a genetic mutation. Corn is a freak of nature, and the plant would most certainly have died out had there not been a human standing by with opposing thumb and fingers to recognize its potential, open its seeds and assure its propagation. Thus began humans' symbiosis with this plant which is now cultivated worldwide.

Though America's native population can be credited with rescuing this plant from its genetic dead end, it was the Scotch-Irish who applied the whiskey-making technology to create the world's first bourbon. Bourbon, incidentally, had no discernible connection to French aristocrats who wore silk stockings, pink satin pants, and ridiculous wigs, except for the fact that they drank it on occasion. Bourbon is a true American beverage.

Evolutionary biologists theorize that the human hand, with its opposing thumb, evolved hand in glove, if you will pardon the expression, with tool-making and the growth of the brain. I believe that this to be only a partial explanation of humans' remarkable physical and mental dexterity.

People in the genteel part of Kentuckiana need to eat occasionally, and when it is not deer season, their preferred source of animal protein comes from swine, in its many savory manifestations.

In my humble opinion, pork is brought to its level of perfection by slicing off a generous hunk of tenderloin, exposing it hickory and cherry smoke for many hours, and finally finishing it off on a charcoal grill. Some people prefer to beat the tenderloin flat with a mallet, roll it in bread crumbs, and drop it into a deep fryer.

German immigrants, of course, made sausages and patés from the lowly oinkers, which they stretched with oats, blood, sawdust, and other fillers. The Amish make a breakfast loaf from hearts, livers and brains, called "Scrapple." Pig parts not suitable even for sausage-making found their way into human stomachs by other means. (Some people are happy to eat "pig's knuckle," and even pig tail.) Germans are a frugal lot.

Among the Scotch-Irish, pork barbeque (frequently abbreviated "BBQ") reigns supreme. To give them credit, BBQ usually begins with a respectable cut of the animal: the shoulder (which inexplicably is called the "butt"). Most frequently, the butt is smoked and/or slow-cooked, and then shellacked with a "sauce" made from high fructose corn syrup, tomato paste and spices which can sometimes set the mouth ablaze. The sauce helps to disguise the connective tissue, and the spices will frequently mask the fact that the meat may be well past its prime.

But among the upper classes in Kentuckiana it is the cured and aged ham. Cured and aged ham is less prone to manipulation, and therefore, I believe, safer to eat, as long as one does not suffer from hypertension, and remains hydrated.

Regardless of how it is served, pork must be accompanied by corn bread, corn muffins, corn pancakes, corn on the cob, creamed corn, corn chowder, corn grits, or corn in some other edible iteration. Then there's caramel corn for dessert. Add to that the fact that pigs are fattened on cracked corn and corn meal, and you can begin to appreciate the importance of corn in our diet.

One can find the finest Kentuckiana hams in the so-called "Ham Belt" near Princeton and Bremen, in western Kentucky. Of the top five country ham producers, as declared by *Bon Appetit* Magazine, three of them—Father's Country Hams, Broadbent Country Hams, and Colonel Bill Newsom's Aged Country Hams—can be found in the "Ham Belt." Jane and I took a road trip there to sample some of the best. She was on assignment for a magazine; I was simply there for the gustatory experience.

On the way, we passed through the town of Leitchfield (pronounced "Leech-field," as in your septic disposal system), and since it was lunch time, we decided to seek out a local eatery. We settled on a place called Sandy's.

Upon first impression, it appeared that we had stumbled upon another pedestrian greasy spoon in rural Kentuckiana, replete with a rotating pie display, offering the usual beef Manhattans, patty melts and chicken-fried whatevers, transported to your table by a painted waitress named Myrtle sporting a beehive hairdo. You get the idea. That was our first impression of Sandy's, and it was exactly what we had hoped to find.

But as we settled into our vinyl booth, with seats split from assaults by countless porcine Kentuckiana backsides, we quickly noticed that EVERYONE in the restaurant was smoking, including the waitress, who had a cigarette dangling from her lips as she brought our menus. Our table had an ashtray, something I had not seen in a restaurant for at least a decade.

As a child growing up around chain smokers, I became acutely aware that I was born with a peculiar talent. Wherever I happened to be, smoke from any lit cigarette nearby would always make its way to my nostrils, by the shortest possible route, with very little dilution. I tried moving, only to find that the tendrils of smoke would immediately shift direction and hunt me down. Cigarette smoke is irresistibly attracted to me.

On that day, Jane and I discovered that I still possessed this remarkable trait. To our chagrin, the couple at the table next to us were both smoking during their meal, each pausing between bites of food to take drags from Marlboros. As each Marlboro burned down into a stub, they would light a new one with the smoldering butt of the old, and then allow the old butt to die a slow, natural death. Thus, at any given time, there were up to four lit cigarettes in the ashtray of the table for two next to us. All of that smoke was making its way to our table.

This made our meal at Sandy's the most unpleasant we have encountered in a very long time. We exited the restaurant as quickly as we could fetch the check from our nicotine-addicted waitress. Our clothes stank for hours after that.

And this is how I acquired a deeper understanding of curing ham by smoke.

People in Kentuckiana smoke. It's the law. It is only natural to cure your favorite meat with smoke, though not necessarily employing tobacco to do it.

The preferred way to cure ham in Kentuckiana is with hickory smoke, brown sugar and brine, over the course of several months. The top makers of cured ham each have their secret recipes, just as Colonel Sanders had his secret herbs and spices. Ham-curers are therefore reticent to disclose those secrets, choosing instead to describe the curing process in as general terms as possible, eager only to wax eloquent as to how their final product beats the competition.

29. Nothing's wasted.

One of the producers we visited was another Kentucky Colonel, of Bill Newsome's Aged Country Hams. It boasted a delightful storefront in downtown Princeton, an authentic 19th century delicatessen/country store, with lots of sugary treats and old stuff on display. As Jane interviewed the proprietor, I stole away and explored the building which, despite its age, had survived intact. One of Newsom's signature products is called "Preacher's Ham," so named by a customer, Betsy Hooks, who served it to evangelists visiting her Baptist minister husband.

Newsome's hams are coveted all over the world, particularly at Christmas time. I wondered silently if they would someday be selling smoked goose, or turkey, to customers celebrating Hanukkah or the end of Ramadan.

Jane and I also visited Harper's Country Hams in nearby Clinton, where we were treated to a private tour of the operation. The aging/curing process is laborious, capital-intensive and time-consuming, so the best country ham does not come cheap. There's a strikingly sweet smell to hams curing in a Kentuckiana smokehouse shed, much like the aroma that greets you in a bourbon barrel aging barn. Like bourbon, there's the "Angel's Share." A lot of evaporation occurs during the curing and aging process, slimming down the hams so they are not so . . . hammy.

Jane and I left "Ham Country" calorically fulfilled, but not victims of gluttony. But something happened to us before we reached the Ohio River on the way home. We both became afflicted by a powerful thirst, requiring us to stop for bottled water at no fewer than two different convenience stores, where we had to wait in line behind people buying cigarettes, lottery tickets and oversized fountain drinks in polystyrene containers. Any way you cut it, cured ham is salty. Tobacco use, not coincidentally, raises one's appetite for, and tolerance of, salt.

Advice: ditch the cigarette butts, and eat cured ham butts only in moderation.

CHAPTER 16. THE SOUTHEAST

> "If the world comes to an end, I want to be in Cincinnati. Everything comes there ten years later."
> —Mark Twain

About 20 miles east and north of Story is Columbus, an impeccably clean town with a nice collection of historic buildings, architectural/botanical features, and parks and gardens. It fortunately has an enlightened town government dedicated to preserving them. Like Story/Nashville, Columbus sits on the northern fringe of Kentuckiana, at precisely the spot the glacier ran out of gas. To the immediate north of Columbus is flat farmland that is stereotypically Indiana; to the south is hill country. Think of Columbus as a border town.

Columbus is the seat of Bartholomew County, with a fine courthouse and downtown that is typical of the towns which dot Kentuckiana. However, Columbus's main employer is not the government but Cummins Engine Company, a manufacturer of heavy-duty diesel engines. One would expect Columbus to be full of red-neck factory workers as a consequence, and it is. However, Cummins has grown to become a global company, and one increasingly sees swarthy engineer/management types from places like India and China. Thus, Columbus is also a window to America's demographic future.

Though Columbus lacks a real university, it does have three breweries, one winery, and a few decent schools. Except for the fact that Mike Pence was born and raised here, Columbus is an attractive place to settle down.

As one turns south and east of Columbus, there's Vernon, a diminutive town of 318 people that serves as the seat of Jennings County. Its courthouse and flanking storefronts are typical of Kentuckiana and worth a look. Jane and I stopped to gawk at the courthouse one day and struck up a conversation a kindly man who, it turned out, was the sitting Circuit Court Judge. He proved to be a treasure trove of local history.

Vernon was once a stop on the so-called Underground Railroad, which spirited black slaves from the South to friendlier places in the North. I'm proud to say that German immigrants were among those most opposed to the institution of slavery, and many of the people inhabiting the tiny towns and farmhouses of Kentuckiana who gave refuge to fleeing slaves were my kinfolk.

Kaiser Wilhelm II, and then Hitler, gave Germans a bad rap in America. There are slightly more people of German than English ancestry in this country, but you wouldn't know it because a lot of them anglicized their names after 1918 and made heroic efforts to blend in. Virtually every large Kentuckiana town had a German-language newspaper before 1918. German is as American as, well, hot dogs and apple pie.

Today, cities like Indianapolis and Cincinnati have sizable African-American populations, due in some part to the concerted effort of bringing these people north to freedom. Since Indiana was a non-slave state, crossing the Ohio River did make a difference, at least until 1865, when the 13th Amendment was passed by the requisite majority of states which then comprised the Union.

The further one travels south and east of Story, the more one begins to feel the presence of Cincinnati. Bengals and Reds bumper stickers appear with greater frequency. Small town newspapers begin to report stuff from Cincinnati. Cincinnati straddles the Kentuckiana/Ohiana border, and its cultural presence if felt well within Kentuckiana.

This puts Greensburg in an odd position. It is located half way between Cincinnati and Indianapolis, comparable cities most respects. Greensburg itself is dominated by a large Japanese automobile assembly plant, which management placed there years ago for the dual purpose of avoiding labor unions and black people.

Greensburg looks like any other Kentuckiana small town, with a town square dominated by an elegant courthouse, faced with 19th century brick storefronts. The courthouse, which serves as the seat of Decatur County's government, has a tree growing out of the top. Courthouse officials noticed a sprig growing there in the 1870s and decided to cultivate it. Successive generations have worked to keep it alive. People in Greensburg are easily amused.

Greensburg, oddly, has a fine country restaurant known as "Storie's," facing that courthouse. It's offered authentic country cooking for decades and has reached iconic status. When traveling southeastern Kentuckiana, it is very easy to have lunch at Storie's and dinner at Story.

Not far from Greensburg is Oldenburg, just three miles off the Batesville exit on I-74. If I ever move away from Story for the purpose of residing some place other than a graveyard, I suspect that it will be to Oldenburg. My love affair with this town dates back to 1986, when I made a quixotic, albeit unsuccessful, attempt to save a Franciscan monastery from an ignominious end.

Oldenburg was settled in 1837 by German immigrants from an identically-named town in Lower Saxony. The early settlers quickly established a community that bore the unmistakable imprint of its Teutonic roots and Catholic faith. These were my people. Frugal, hard-working and hard-drinking. Religious they were, but not too sanctimonious about it.

Oldenburg is located about an hour's drive northwest of Cincinnati, in the rolling hills of Franklin County. It sits on the eastern fringe of Kentuckiana, bordering Ohiana. About 675 people now inhabit the village, a great number of whom are senior citizens bearing German surnames. This population sustains no fewer than three taverns, which would not be possible if the settlers had been Methodist or Mormon.

Foremost among those taverns is The Brauhaus, where one may enjoy a meal of fried chicken and coleslaw, washed down with a local German-style lager. If the Cincinnati Reds or Bengals happen to be playing, it is a certainty that the tavern's only television will be tuned to the game.

Despite its diminutive size, Oldenburg possesses a magnificent number of ecclesiastical buildings: a cathedral that could nearly accommodate every one of the town's residents; a modest stone church that dates back to the 1830s; a convent/chapel for Franciscan sisters established by Mother Theresa Hackelmeyer in 1851, and a girls' boarding school that has the look, and feel, of an elite European university campus. All such structures are brick, with slate roofs, adorned with leaded glass, in the German Renaissance Revival style. Seven spires pierce the sky, earning the town its nickname, the "Village of Spires."

The entire town of Oldenburg was placed on the National Register of Historic Places in 1983. Even the streets bear German names (*Hauptstrasse*—Main Street, *Perlenstrasse*—Pearl Street, *Wasserstrasse*—Water Street). When one visits the town today, one feels transported to Germany, at about the time of Germany's belated unification in 1871.

There's a large graveyard in Oldenburg, too, where hundreds of Franciscan nuns have been laid to rest for nearly two centuries. This proved to be an irresistible attraction to Jane on our most recent visit.

30. Living a clean life doesn't necessarily equate to longevity.

Jane forced me to walk past the many rows of graves (old cemeteries are her thing), each marked by an identical white stone cross. The nuns were laid to rest in impeccably straight rows, strictly following the chronological date of death. On the day we last visited, at the end of the line was a hole dug for its latest addition.

Since nuns are forbidden to marry, their graves were marked with their maiden names, all of them German, each cross faithfully recording the date of birth and death. Some of those nuns had lived impressively long lives. One of them was sister Angela Benedict, who died just short of her 105th birthday on March 29, 2015. In my mind, this graveyard perfectly evinces the German penchant for structure and order.

Despite their common language, culture and ancestry, Germans have historically not gotten along very well, unless geography or family ties compel them to consistently drink beer together. It is said that if you place three sober Germans into a room, they will quickly organize nine different singing clubs, none of which will talk to one another. When a German becomes afflicted with Alzheimer's disease, he forgets everything but the grudge. Jane's favorite—obviously directed at me—is that you can always tell a German, but you can't tell him much.

The town of Oldenburg today would have been even more impressive had an officious, arrogant and mortifyingly obese Archbishop from Indianapolis not decreed that one of the town's most magnificent buildings be torn down. It was a senseless act of vandalism.

Now I will rant.

The culprit's name was Archbishop Edward O'Meara (officially to be addressed as "Your Excellency"). For reasons which mystify me even today, His Excellency decreed that the old Franciscan Monastery, once the headquarters of the Franciscan Order of monks in the United States, had to be razed.

True, the old Monastery had stood empty for a number of years, but the building was sound and suitable for rehabilitation, and a local preservation organization was keen on keeping it maintained at no cost to the Archdiocese of Indianapolis (which owned it) or the local parish (which managed it), until something useful could be done with it. As a young lawyer, I fought first to challenge the granting of a demolition permit, and secondly, to appeal to His Excellency's powers of reason. I failed on both accounts.

The old Monastery was an imposing brick and slate structure, occupying the better part of a block, also built in the Renaissance Revival style. It consisted mostly of small rooms, called "cells," for the monks to sleep and pray. There were also a number of common areas, for recreation and dining.

It even had a swimming pool. It was incumbent upon all parties to seek, in good faith, an alternative to turning it into rubble.

In a matter of weeks, our civic-minded locals were able to entice some Catholic investors from Cincinnati. I assisted these investors in preparing and submitting a purchase offer to His Excellency, proposing to buy (read: pay good money for) the Monastery, for the purpose of converting it into a Catholic retirement home to be staffed with Franciscan sisters. That seemed like a win-win situation to me. I waited, in confidence, to receive an acceptance, or at least a counter-offer, from His Excellency.

But His Excellency had made his mind up: The building had to go. And down it came, just as the "Village of Spires" was celebrating its sesquicentennial (at an event, ironically, named thè *Freudenfest*, or "Festival of Joy"). (The *Freudenfest* has since grown to become Kentuckiana's largest German beer festival.)

I am told that the pompous, porcine prelate reached his decision after considerable "prayer." Had God really instructed His Excellency to turn down a perfectly good offer, demolish a priceless artifact with no plans to construct anything in its place, and stick the local parish with the bill for its demolition? I think not.

The First Vatican Council defined the "doctrine" of papal infallibility in 1870, just as Germany was uniting in a secular body politic and the German people coming to terms with their Catholic–Lutheran bipolar disease. As an alternative explanation of his odd behavior, I would submit to you that His Excellency had no such beatific vision but instead mistakenly believed that some of this infallibility from the First Vatican Council had rubbed off on him.

Today, there's a vacant lot where the Monastery once stood, a gaping hole ripped from the heart of this historic community. Some of my disgusted fellow preservationists left the local parish, or even the Church itself, for good. It took several years before I could again visit Oldenburg and feel good about what's still there. I give O'Meara a lot of credit for making me the broken, curmudgeonly old cynic that I am today.

If I ever become afflicted with Alzheimer's disease, this is one grudge that I will never forget.

End of rant.

Cincinnati straddles the Kentuckiana–Ohiana divide, carrying attributes of each. Germans are ubiquitous in both cultures. In Kentuckiana, the Germans tend to look and act like Germans. In Ohiana and places east, the Germans tend to look and act like ordinary, boring white people from the suburbs.

Not far from Oldenburg, also in Franklin County, is the tiny village of Metamora, founded in 1838. The town was once a stop along the Whitewater Canal, which connected to Batesville. (Batesville, by the way, is the country's leading producer of funeral caskets.) But since few things move by barge these days, Metamora's population has dwindled to a mere 188 at last count. It's a place worth visiting for a few minutes at least, to take in its storefront architecture and the old canal locks. Metamora is the location of Indiana's oldest water-powered grist mill. There are also a few shops selling candies, candles and, of course, caramel corn. The place is deserted November through April.

The Ohio River between Cincinnati and Louisville gave birth to, and continues to sustain, the culture of Southeast Kentuckiana. Mark Twain captured America's literary imagination with his stories of runaway boys and slaves, and steamboats, on the mighty Mississippi. The Ohio, of course, eventually empties into the Mississippi, so its contribution to this part of America's culture is more than metaphorical.

As a young boy in the Pittsburgh area who enthusiastically read *The Adventures of Huckleberry Finn*, I once sealed a letter into a bottle and threw it into a tributary of the Ohio. (To be more accurate, I threw the bottle into the Youghiogheny River, which empties into the Monongahela River at a place called McKeesport, which in turn joins the Allegheny River at Pittsburgh to form the Ohio. You could wade across the Youghiogheny at the point I committed this act of eco-terrorism.) In that letter, I promised the finder a reward of $1 for contacting me, a handsome incentive in my mind, and nearly all of the money I had to my name.

For weeks, I anxiously awaited a response, imagining I would hear from someone in Cincinnati, Louisville, Paducah, Memphis, or even New Orleans. The answer eventually came, from a kid about my age who lived just four miles downstream, in Boston, on my side of McKeesport. I paid him his dollar.

In retrospect, I'm amazed that anyone would distinguish my bottle from ordinary flotsam in the Youghiogheny those days. That river was little more than an open sewer in the late 1960s, so I was extraordinarily lucky.

I will resist the urge to write much about Cincinnati, the gateway to Kentuckiana and the situs of a place called "Over the Rhine," except to rave and rant, respectively, about its two grand hotels, the Netherland Plaza and the Cincinnatian. Both were built in the tradition of late 19th and early 20th century edifice-hubris, which littered them across America, ultimately to be humbled by the Great Depression, the Second World War, and America's enduring love affair with the automobile.

The Netherland Plaza, inauspiciously completed in 1931 to coincide with the peak of the Great Depression, is a stunning architectural gem in the French Art Deco Style. It is a behemoth, often referred to as a "city within a city," full of shops, offices, retail stores, offices, banquet halls and, of course, restaurants. The commercial portion of the building, known as the Carew Tower, features prominently in Cincinnati's skyline today. If I were a lawyer practicing in Cincinnati, that's where I would have my office.

Jane and I dined in the Orchids Palm Court in utter opulence. When we sent back a glass-pour wine that had turned (it happens even in the best of places), we caught the attention of its sommelier, who then insisted that we indulge in a customized food/wine pairing. It didn't take much arm-twisting for us to agree. The meal—and the atmosphere—were phenomenal. Like the Seelbach in Louisville, the Netherland Plaza is managed by Hilton, which assures a consistent level of service, if you can stomach the stupid uniforms. There's an impressive banquet hall upstairs, known as the "Hall of Mirrors."

The Cincinnatian was constructed in 1882, in the Second Empire style. It is large, but a fraction of the size of the Netherland Plaza. Originally called the "Palace Hotel," it served as the meeting point of Cincinnati's elite for decades. After a period of decline, the Cincinnatian received a $25 million renovation in 1987. Unfortunately, the renovation did much to destroy the original character of the building.

31. Wheeler Homestead at Story: A restoration

At this point, I will pause to clarify the difference between a "renovation" and a "restoration." The former is usually an extensive re-build that often occurs when a historic building is repurposed (as, for example, when an old warehouse is converted into loft apartments). The latter is much more conservative, an effort to wipe away the grime and make a place shine like new. At Story, we renovated the Old Mill, converting it from a grain mill into an overnight accommodation. This allowed us to take considerable liberties during construction. In contrast, we restored the Doc Story and Wheeler homesteads, to make them look original.

The Cincinnatian's $25 million face lift was a renovation, and a bad one at that. The building's outer skin survives relatively intact, but inside, the building has been hollowed out to create an atrium, giving one the impression of having just walked into a 1980s Embassy Suites Hotel. It was a severe disappointment, and inexcusable. The Cincinnatian has always been a hotel. It needed to be restored, not renovated.

Edifice complex consumed Cincinnatians well into the late 20th century. Prominent among them was Charles Keating, Jr., a sanctimonious Catholic who, at the behest of Richard Nixon, wrote a not so convincing "study" linking pornography to the collapse of civilization. That earned him the respect of five U.S. senators who successfully interfered with federal banking regulators who foresaw the collapse of Keating's Lincoln Savings and Loan in 1989, and with it a number of grandiose real estate projects. Keating's financial shenanigans eventually cost taxpayers $2 billion and landed him in federal prison, where he could then lecture his fellow inmates about the evils of pornography.

Keating's son, Charles Keating III, was a teammate of mine at IU. Charlie III made the 1976 Olympic Swimming Team; I did not.

The Ohio River's serpentine journey west from Cincinnati is a joy to take, even if one must do it by motorcar. There's a road which more or less tracks the river on its north side, designated the "Ohio River Scenic Byway," from the Indiana border near Cincinnati, to the Illinois border beyond Evansville. It is worthy of a multi-day trip, one that traverses many of the counties, towns and territories described in chapters of this book entitled "Southwest," "South" and "Southeast."

Traveling west from Cincinnati (judiciously avoiding Lawrenceburg and its tacky casino), the road will take you through several ancient villages, including Vevay, which gave birth to America's first winery. Yes, this is wine country, and the southern fringe of the "Indiana Uplands American Viticultural Area."

Six of these wineries have created their own "Indiana Wine Trail," which partially tracks this scenic byway, at least until the AVA ends. My favorite among them is Ertel Cellars, which has a nice combination tasting room and restaurant, and several estate-grown whites. The Ohio River has exposed an impressive number of fossils, and Ertel has built a limestone wall at the entrance to its tasting room with countless exposed marine fossils. (The so-called "Cincinnati Arch" in this area is a broad structural uplift of sedimentary rock formed in the late Ordovician through the Devonian Period.) This ought to persuade even the most narrow-minded fundamentalist that the Earth is much older than 6,000 years, but facts don't seem to matter much to people who have their minds made up.

Mercifully, I have encountered very few evangelicals at wineries.

As Kentuckiana river towns go, Madison is about the loveliest, located about halfway between Cincinnati and Louisville. Madison was platted in 1810, and quickly developed into a major commercial hub. But its days were numbered. River traffic declined as railroads were built connecting Louisville, Indianapolis and Cincinnati, bypassing Madison.

Madison ironically was the site of Indiana's first railroad, the Madison & Indianapolis Railroad, which went into operation in 1836. But it went into decline and was sold at foreclosure 1862. Madison ceased to be an important commercial hub after the Civil War, as railroads replaced river (and canal) freight traffic. And when automobiles and lorries replaced trains, it didn't occur to anyone to build an interstate highway nearby. And when air transportation came along, no one thought to build an airport, either. Thus, the river gave birth to Madison, but ironically, it was isolation which put it into stasis.

The city has many remarkable architectural treasures, including the Lanier Mansion, built in 1844. Its downtown bears some remarkable brick storefronts dating from the mid-19th century. In 2006, the majority of Madison's downtown, 133 blocks *in toto*, was designated as the largest contiguous historic landmark district in the United States.

Madison's roughly 12,000 inhabitants cannot begin to fill all that space, so the town today feels almost deserted. Real estate is bizarrely cheap there, due to the law of supply and demand. The key architectural fortresses seem to be well-maintained, but a good number of the second-tier buildings have slid into disrepair. Two friends of mine have independently invested in old homes in Madison, and if that is evidence of a trend, then Madison has a bright future. The problem is that Madison is a long way from anywhere important.

The city boasts three wineries as well as the oldest tavern in Indiana, the Broadway. There are several nice B&Bs in town, and Jane and I stayed in two of the loveliest among them, the Whitehall and the Iron Gate.

The Whitehall, on the west end of the Historic District, is really more of a museum than a B&B. It is an antebellum colonial revival mansion packed to the gills with rare artifacts, including a grand piano with a sound board peculiarly bent at a right angle to its keyboard, enabling it to be parked into a small space. It was a practical design if space is at a premium, but wholly impractical given the instrument's function. A grand piano needs to be in an open ballroom, not a closet or stairwell, to appreciate its full effect. That's why so few of them were built and why they are so rare today.

The Iron Gate, on the east end of the Historic District, occupies an imposing brick structure built in the Federal style, in 1840. I resolved to count the fireplaces but became distracted by the ornate woodwork and pocket doors. The Inn's a comfortable stroll from what passes as Madison's commercial district, and has antebellum urban feel to it.

For all of its lovely architecture, Madison is sorely lacking in fine restaurants. Given the choices, Jane and I chose to dine at the Key West Shrimp House, which we appreciated for its 1950s Howard Johnson's motif. This eatery evinces Kentuckianans' penchant for placing restaurants offering saltwater fish next to any available body of fresh water, just for the appearance of authenticity. The food, all of which was fried and heavily salted, had us both reaching for the vitamin E and water bottles.

Wherever you may roam in Madison, you're never far from the river. The town is a thin rectangle fronting the river, with streets running roughly parallel to it. This configuration was made necessary by the fact that this part of Kentuckiana is hilly. The town's built on a small alluvial plain at the riverfront, and one not need go far from the river's north bank to encounter steep hills, beautiful but impractical for development. As one can imagine, the townspeople have endured some nasty flooding over the years.

To the west of Madison is the Clifty Falls State Park, a small (1,400 acre) park set atop a hill that overlooks the Ohio River. It's an imposing view, obstructed only by a coal-fired electric generating plant with an even more imposing smokestack. If the brain could download Photoshop and paint out the plant, one could enjoy a breathtaking view of southeastern Kentuckiana from there.

Clifty Falls has a medium-sized lodge run by the Indiana Department of Natural Resources, which was built on a bluff overlooking the mighty Ohio and aforementioned power plant. The lodge has the look, feel and odor that one encounters in any government-run institution, including VA hospitals and prisons. Until very recently, Indiana was too prudish to sell alcohol at its many fine state parks, rendering the experience even less enjoyable for taxpayers and less profitable for the state.

Indiana is also the only state in the country that does not permit carry-out liquor sales on Sundays. Yes, it is totally legal for us to ply a Harley rider in the Story Inn's tavern with shots of 151 rum and send him out on the road without a helmet, but we will face a serious fine for sending him home with a six-pack.

A bit further west of Clifty Falls is Hanover College, founded in 1827 by John Finley Crowe, a Presbyterian minister. Hanover is Indiana's oldest private college, and it enjoys both an excellent academic reputation as well as a breathtaking view of the Ohio Valley not obstructed by a coal-fired power plant.

The most spectacular view of the Ohio from this scenic byway is, in my opinion, at a place called the Overlook Restaurant near Leavenworth. Leavenworth's a bit west of Louisville, so it's a real journey from Madison/ Hanover, and perhaps best seen when visiting Louisville or places to the South. The Overlook serves mediocre food and looks to be badly in need of a cleaning. But the restaurant sits atop a hill, with a majestic view of where the river makes an "oxbow" in its course, allowing one to see up to 10 miles of river, upstream and downstream. Jane and I found ourselves lingering over some fried perch just to take it all in.

At least perch is native to local bodies of fresh water.

PART III: Journeys Beyond Reality

Chapter 17. Candide meets Pangloss

> "It's even harder for the average ape to be-
> lieve that he has descended from man."
>
> —H. L. Mencken

The Bible is the world's most widely published and circulated book.

We find copies of the Gideon Bible spontaneously appearing in the Story Inn's guest rooms. As with any unexplained empirical fact, one first needs a plausible and testable hypothesis to explain it. One might hypothesize that these Bibles appeared out of thin air, by divine intervention. But that theory would be impossible to test, so I have developed another working theory: that someone keeps dropping them in our rooms in an apparent effort to save a lost soul or two. I will be able to confirm that hypothesis once I catch a Gideon in the act of Bible-planting.

In Kentuckiana, every household has a Bible, too. That's another law. Quite a number of people here actually read it, and quite a number of those take it literally.

The Bible maintains that God created the universe in six days, a labor that taxed even his omnipotent powers, requiring him to rest on the seventh. When the earth's crust solidified some 4.5 billion years ago, a "day" was much shorter than it is today, owing to the Moon's tidal effects—perhaps nine hours long. You can understand why God got tuckered out. But the Bible also assures us that the universe is only 6,000 years old, so if you buy the biblical account, there was no earth 4.5 billion years ago.

These and many other biblical pronouncements contradict observable facts. That's a real problem.

My father, who was possessed of scientific training as well as a three-digit IQ, clung to his Catholicism until he went to his grave. To reconcile his religion with observable fact, he concluded that the Bible should be read allegorically and metaphorically. A "day" could equate to a couple of billion years. "Creation" could have been the Big Bang, set in motion by God 13 billion years ago. You get the picture.

In Kentuckiana, most people take the opposite approach. They accept the Bible as gospel (pardon the pun), and then tailor the scientific facts to fit it. That's the approach they take at the Creation Museum in Petersburg, Kentucky, a product of the religious zealotry of Ken Ham, as well as generous tax credits and public subsidies from the Commonwealth of Kentucky and people like you and me. Its mission statement: "The Creation Museum exists to point today's culture back to the authority of Scripture and proclaim the gospel message." In other words, it exists for the purpose of molding science to fit Ham's literal interpretation of the story of creation found in the Judeo-Christian Bible.

A visit to the Creation Museum has been on my "bucket list" for a very long time, and now that I've undertaken to write this account of life as a *Freidenker* in Kentuckiana, it was incumbent upon me to make it happen.

The Museum sits just southwest of Cincinnati, a mere six miles from the north Kentucky airport that serves the metro area, but solidly on this side of the Ohiana/Kentuckiana border. Jane refused to accompany me to the Museum, probably because she doesn't like people who drive SUVs with stick families on the back window. Maybe she's afraid of them, because they all carry guns. (As a Progressive, Jane is prone to making stereotypes.)

On the day I visited, the parking lot was about half-filled with vehicles, three-quarters of which were SUVs, and a stunning one-half of which bore license plates from outside of Kentuckiana. Some of the SUVs had stick-families pasted on the back window, but fewer than I would have expected. Remarkably, there was only one pick-up truck, and it did not have a gun rack. There were a couple of cars with a chrome Christian fish symbol, but none bearing a statement in support of the Second Amendment. So much for the "clinger" stereotype.

The Creation Museum most emphatically looks like a museum. It does not have the trappings of a church. The main hall sits next to a lovely stocked pond populated with swan and geese, surrounded by well-tended gardens. I expected to find a theme park, much like nearby King's Island, where I spent one intolerable day each summer for several consecutive years until my four children thought better of it. Mercifully, there were no rides at the Creation Museum, though it did have a petting zoo and a zip line, and there was an abundance of sugary confections and drinks for sale.

I paid the $30 admission fee to a courteous attendant, grabbed some literature, and began to look around. There was a gift shop/bookstore at the entrance to the exhibit, which I found to be annoying, but besides the admission fee and the presence of so much religious schlock for sale, no one came by to shake me down for a "contribution."

Now for the demographics. The crowd that day at the Creation Museum was surprisingly well kempt and well dressed, and no one looked to be a meth addict. I didn't see a single tattoo (though I may have missed some because people were modestly dressed). A surprising number of the visitors that day were children, being shepherded by parents and/or Sunday school teachers. One group were clearly Mennonites (not Amish, since they arrived by car).

The Museum is dedicated only to the first chapter of the Bible: the story of creation, the punishment of Adam and Eve, the great flood and Noah's Ark, and the Tower of Babel. As you enter the main room, you see an improbable display of humans playfully coexisting with dinosaurs. The Museum is nondenominational, meaning it doesn't push the variations of any particular Christian sect. All Christian sects have their take on the creation, and the Creation Museum glossed over that with some degree of tact.

Being limited to Genesis, they spared us the science behind the improbable immaculate conception of Christ, his improbable miracles (my favorite one is turning water into wine), his death and improbable resurrection, his improbable ascension into heaven, and the improbable events that the Bible says will occur when God improbably beams up his loyal followers and leaves the rest of us to suffer the consequences of our non-belief when he decrees that our lease on this earth is over.

There were bones and fossils. Lots of them. And videos.

I watched a candid video in which two paleontologists were unearthing a dinosaur skeleton in Montana. The first explained the find in standard scientific terms: that the whatever-saur had died some 100 million years ago, was covered in mud and then fossilized. The second then said, "I prefer to start with a different beginning," and then he went on to explain that the poor whatever-saur had died and was covered by water and debris in the great biblical flood that occurred about 2,350 years before the birth of Christ, and had then become fossilized. Sorely missing was a peer-review third scientist to ask scientist no. 2 why he would assume that there was a great flood about 4,366 years ago, and what evidence he had for that.

It is the nature of science to question everything, including both the Bible and doctrinaire religious teachings. This, of course, has put religion into conflict with advancing science. The clashes in the past were not so cordial. Giordano Bruno was burned at the stake; Galileo Galilei avoided a similar fate when he recanted. In all fairness to the Creation Museum, no one seemed eager to persecute scientists, and impressively, in one of the video displays, it appears that the Creation Museum has even come to terms with the fact that the earth revolves around the sun, not vice versa. I call that progress.

One display attempted to debunk the various methods by which scientists attempt to date fossils and rocks over geologic time, using different radioactive isotopes (a technique known as "radiometric dating"). The display correctly showed that each method derived a different age for the bone in question. The differences, of course, were due to the varying half-lives of the decaying isotopes, but this detail was conveniently ignored.

The problem here is that all techniques showed the dinosaur bone to be many millions, not thousands, of years old, and from a geologic perspective, they were all in the same ballpark. A prudent scientist would have taken the average, which would have dated the bone to the Jurassic period, and then looked for geologic evidence to fix a more accurate date. Thus, this display did nothing to add credibility to the biblical account that the earth, and its animals and plants, all came into existence only 6,000 years ago while God was on a six-day creative tear.

When God became disgusted with human wickedness and decided to exterminate us in a flood, save for Noah's virtuous family of eight, he instructed Noah to build an ark. The ark was a behemoth of its day, measuring 300 cubits long by 50 cubits wide by 30 cubits high (a "cubit" being the distance between a man's elbow and finger tips, or about 18 inches). However, the whole contraption would fit comfortably on the deck of one of today's container ships.

Johan Huibers, a Dutch businessman, built a full-scale replica of the ark in 2012, though he took a shortcut by welding together the hulls of 25 river barges. He then shrouded the flotilla in Scandinavian pinewood for authenticity (the Bible called for "gopher wood"). Huiber's floating, albeit not seaworthy, "Bible Museum" contains numerous familiar plastic animals plucked from kiddie books, sleeping quarters, a theatre, restaurant and conference facilities. Pretty impressive, until one puts it next to a Nimitz-class aircraft carrier.

Into this ark, Noah deposited male and female of every sexually-reproducing species on earth (and presumably only one of each asexually-reproducing species on earth) to preserve them from God's collateral damage. The rest were destined to become fossils, or hydrocarbons.

There are at least 10 million different species alive on this planet today. (Evidence shows that a great many more than that have gone extinct over geologic time—perhaps 100 times as many— but we'll ignore that for the moment.) Let's assume that Noah's world was similarly endowed with species, and further, that half of those could survive immersion in water for any significant period of time. Thus, Noah would only have needed to load up those creatures which could not swim away unscathed. That's still a pretty packed vessel—five million species.

In all fairness to Noah, a good number of these species were microscopic, requiring little more than petri dishes for transport. A handful of topsoil contains about a billion microbes. But there's no mention in the scriptures of petri dishes, or how Noah went about the herculean task of making sure that he collected a specimen of every single microbe there was to be found on the planet. Some of them live only inside glaciers, in fumaroles at Yellowstone Park, or in brine seas.

Likewise, plants could more easily be transported by seeds. Bill Gates, the Rockefeller Foundation, Monsanto, Syngenta and the Norwegian government have jointly funded the "doomsday seed bank" near the village of Longyearbyan, on Spitsbergen Island, to protect and preserve the seeds of three million food crop varieties. It took the wealth of these actors just to preserve the genomes of a tiny portion of the plant kingdom. Did Noah bring in potted palms or just seeds? The scripture is silent on this point.

A good number of species would have been insects, making the ark a pretty buggy place, I would imagine. Scientists estimate that there are some 22,000 species of ants alone. (Query, as eusocial insects, would one drone and queen of each species have sufficed? Probably not.) Conceivably, some of these critters could have been transported effectively as larvae, pupae or even eggs, saving space in the ark. It would have been very helpful for Noah to have had a few tanks of liquid nitrogen on board for cryogenic preservation. Once again, the scripture is silent on this point.

In God's infinite compassion, it would have been nice if he would have allowed Noah to leave a few troublemakers behind, such as the HIV virus, as well as the bugs which cause malaria, small pox, Ebola, Marburg, influenza, botulism, bubonic plague, yellow fever, dengue, polio, anthrax, meningitis, syphilis, measles, mumps, and the heartbreak of psoriasis.

Since Ken Ham and his disciples believe that dinosaurs coexisted with humans, we must assume that Noah had to make room for them, too. Paleontologists have identified 700 different species of dinosaurs so far, ranging in size from that of a chicken to a large house. Argentinosaurus alone was 120 feet from head to tail, and weighed almost 100 tons. I would assume that the amorous pair which made that journey found accommodations to be a bit cramped, and malodorous. The insects on board, at least, would have been praising God.

By necessity, Noah must have been a stern captain of his vessel to keep his cargo from devouring each other.

During the past couple of centuries alone we've seen the dodo bird, ivory billed woodpecker, Carolina parakeet, passenger pigeon and countless other species go extinct at the hands of humans. It would seem that God, being omniscient, would surely have spared Noah the trouble of loading these onto his vessel if they had already been marked for extinction.

In addition to transporting five million species, this ark had to hold enough food to tide them over until the flood waters receded. That would have presented a formidable logistical challenge for Noah, though recycling the waste from the dinosaurs alone would probably have sustained a good number of the arthropods.

Noah, we are told, pulled off this feat, and gave an offering to God of one unfortunate hooved creature in gratitude when the ark finally came to rest on dry land, leaving us to assume that this entire species went extinct as a result of Noah's obsequious gesture. Perhaps it was a unicorn that paid with its life that day.

Except for the unicorn, those lucky creatures that poured out of Noah's ark became fruitful and multiplied and colonized the earth as we know it today. Noah's family set out in different directions, and quickly developed into the mélange of racial phenotypes we witness among humans today. All of that happened to us in the past 4,366 years. Nowhere in the Museum was there mention of the Clovis people who roamed Kentuckiana some 13,000 years ago, by the best estimate of anthropologists.

Then there was the matter of species-specific genetic diversity, or lack of it. Only one pair of each sexually reproducing species would have presented a bit of a problem. Succeeding generations would have to breed with siblings, cousins, etc. This happens among humans with alarming frequency in Kentuckiana today, and the results are not pretty. This challenge was not adequately addressed at the Creation Museum.

Another display attacked Charles Darwin, and a nearby one dramatized the Scopes Monkey Trial. Although Scopes was found guilty of teaching evolution in violation of Tennessee's "Butler Act," it was a hollow victory for the fundamentalists, according to the account, since creationism is not taught in most schools today. Curiously, the anti-Darwin display showed a representation of the double-helix, in acknowledgment of the well-known means by which creatures carry and pass on genetic traits. James Watson and Francis Crick discovered the double helix in 1953, which was 28 years after the Scopes trial.

The purpose of the display was to debunk Darwin's contention that we evolved from ape-like creatures. God created us in his own image (albeit imperfectly, requiring him to wipe us out periodically as punishment for our wickedness). We are God's children; we are not apes. The display ignored the rather compelling evidence that we share almost 99% of our genes in common with bonobos, which live in Hippie-like troops south of the Congo River.

Anthropologists have recovered fossilized remains of creatures that seem to bear an even closer resemblance to us. The facts show that we bred with one of them, *Homo neanderthalensis*, rather freely, and today we each carry about 3% Neanderthal genes. None of this was mentioned at the Museum, perhaps because, by mapping genomes, geneticists have determined that Neanderthals became extinct about 54,000 years before God created the world and thus, *ipso facto*, the geneticists got it wrong.

There also was a display of "Lucy," a well-known hominid known as *Australopithecus*. But the Museum dismissed her as just another ape. She nevertheless looked to be more human than many of the knuckle-draggers one sees at the Brown County Fair each summer.

Remarkably, though, the Darwin-debunking display readily acknowledged that species could change by the process of selection, whether naturally or with the influence of people. The Creation Museum does not deny the improvements we have made to crops and livestock by means of selection and, more recently, gene splicing. It fits into God's plan to give us dominion over the earth, to be fruitful, and to multiply.

The anti-Darwin display seemed to focus on one point: that selection can create changes in certain animals and plants, but the process of selection cannot create entirely new animals and plants. A bird cannot become a fish, for example. To illustrate that point, the Creation Museum's display postulated (with a notable lack of scriptural support) that Noah had loaded only one breeding pair of canines onto his ark, and that these were ultimately selected to morph into wolves, foxes, coyotes and, of course, the family dog, all of that change occurring in only the past 4,366 years.

If one accepts the assumption that the earth is a mere 6,000 years old, then, undeniably, a bird cannot be selected to become a fish—at least if one is using science and not magic.

The facts show that simple prokaryotes bobbed around in earth's oceans and tidal pools as far back as 3.6 billion years ago. A billion is a thousand million, and a million is a thousand thousand. That's enough time for prokaryotes to evolve eukaryotes, microbial mats, symbiotes, primitive plants and animals, fish, reptiles, birds, mammals and man. Time matters. In fact, a good portion of this diversity of life has arisen since the so-called "Cambrian Explosion" a mere 540 million years ago, proving that evolution can go into hyper drive when the conditions are right. A paltry 6,000 years won't cut it (even if you add an extra year to account for the first year after Christ's death, which logically is year "0"; evangelicals overlook this).

The Museum even attempts to reconcile certain observed geological facts with the Bible. There was, in fact, a supercontinent called "Pangea," and that continent broke up into the seven continents we observe today. So far so good. However, Pangea came apart as a result of being covered by flood waters 4,366 years ago, not as a result of tectonic heaving occurring over hundreds of millions of years. The Museum did not explain how water could force continents to move, exerting only force from above over a very short period of time. I found the conventional explanation, that continental drift is the result of enormous pressure from below, caused by thermal convection over eons, to be more compelling.

About that flood. The biblical account I read as a Catholic pupil said that it rained for 40 days and 40 nights. The Creation Museum tells a different story. God unleashed a tsunami by opening up a rift in the earth's crust, causing a prodigious amount of water to gush forth and inundate all dry land on earth. The video I saw showed a village of Sumerians looking up in horror as a miles-high wave came to wipe them out for their wicked ways. The Museum ignored the fact that this tsunami would have turned Noah's ark into matchsticks as well.

Below the earth's crust lies the mantle, molten rock which is scorchingly hot and relatively bereft of water. Below that is the core, which is mostly liquid nickel and iron. It would be logical, under the Museum's scenario, that upon opening the earth's crust, God unleashed a pyroclastic flow, not a flood, and that people died as a result of being vaporized, or were buried alive, or, like those unfortunates in Pompeii who sought refuge in cellars, from asphyxiation. Noah's ark would have been burned to a cinder under these conditions.

So let's assume that the Museum is accurate, and that God's weapon of choice was indeed water, and let's assume, further, that the water was not so hot so as to kill the 5 million or so species that could otherwise survive immersion in it, or boil Noah's ark like a poached egg.

That leads to some further unanswered questions. Was it salt water or fresh? And where did it come from?

Most water-dwelling species find a home in either salt or fresh water. Very few of them can cross between them. The biblical account on this point is silent, and so is the Museum's, but I would assume that God sent fresh water so that Noah and his family and barnyard friends could have something to drink. That would lighten his load considerably, unless God provided Noah with a desalination kit.

So let's assume that the water was fresh. That would mean that Noah would have had to make room for corals, hermit crabs and a host of fish that couldn't tolerate fresh water. The ark was already overbooked without them.

So where did this water come from? There's not enough of it on earth to cover all land masses, so clearly, God must have just put it there.

This would have increased the earth's mass significantly, and depending upon how God chose to ladle it on and off, would have wreaked havoc with the earth's rotation. This water mass would have added, at least temporarily, to gravitational pull, thereby altering the ark's displacement in the water (possibly rendering it unstable) and even causing the moon's orbit to decay.

On second thought, maybe God really did send salt water, which would have made the ark more buoyant. But Noah would then have had to make room for perch, guppies and a host of saltwater-intolerant creatures in that already overcrowded ark.

Give the Museum a break. Let's assume that God put his thumb on the globe to keep it spinning steadily and gently pushed the moon into its customary orbit to keep it from careening down to earth as a result of the earth's sudden acquisition of gravitational mass.

The Museum contends that the earth's canyons, like the Grand Canyon that every American ought to place on his or her bucket list to visit, were not created by erosion over millions of years. No, the Grand Canyon was created in just a couple of years, as the flood waters receded.

I've seen floods wreak havoc on roads, bridges, basements, towns, computers and phone systems, and would have to agree that there would be considerable scouring of the earth's surface as God ladled off miles of it all at once, or sucked it out with a straw. But why did he choose to remove it in such a destructive manner, instead of allowing it to gently dissipate, the way a wet towel dries in the sun?

It is not necessary to go any further, if one's objective is simply to kick the legs out from under the Creation Museum. My dad's approach, to twist scripture to fit the facts, seems preferable, if one is determined to cling to the notion that there's a God at all.

Financially, Ken Ham must have done well with the Creation Museum, since he went on to build a $100 million Christian-themed amusement park centered around another life-sized replica of the ark. His "Noah's Ark Theme Park" in Williamstown, Kentucky, opened in 2016. The park is strategically located halfway between Lexington and Cincinnati, and less than an hour's drive from the Creation Museum. It is a very long way from a body of navigable water.

Both attractions are heavily subsidized by taxpayers, earning Ham criticism from secularists everywhere. Personally, I cannot get it out of my head that Ham is proselytizing for profit. It's a P.T. Barnum thing.

I've decided to drop the theme park from my bucket list.

Chapter 18. The Trip of a Lifetime

> "I would like to die on Mars. Just not on impact."
>
> Elon Musk

When Frank and I landed in Brown County, the locals thought we'd come from Mars. Mars is the only planet we know of that is occupied exclusively by robots. Someday, I would like to visit there, to keep the robots company. In some respects, it would be a refreshing change from Brown County. I honestly think I could adapt to life on Mars easier than in Washington, DC.

Mars has more dry land than Earth, so there would be a lot to explore. However, I would have to be content to visit no other place. For practical reasons, it would be a one-way trip.

I still remember vividly watching the Apollo 11 landing, impossibly late at night for a 12-year-old. The fuzzy image of Neil Armstrong stepping from the Lunar Module's pad onto the surface of the Moon, "That's one small step for man . . ." still leaves my skin tingling. Years later, at the Smithsonian, I made sure to touch a moon rock with all 10 fingers. I made my kids do the same.

The first moon landing occurred on July 20, 1969. That was only 66 years after the Wright Brothers' first flight at Kitty Hawk, North Carolina. I seriously discussed the future of space travel with my father, who is still the smartest man I have ever known. We agreed that it would be possible to board a regularly scheduled PanAm flight to lunar bases by the end of the 20th century, and that there would be permanent human colonies on Mars by the spring of 2017.

As Yogi Berra said, "The future ain't what it used to be." We were both guilty of giddy optimism as well as a bit of myopia. We were not alone.

The moon is a mere 384,400 kilometers away (let's use the metric system, since Mars is decidedly outside of the United States). I've driven cars further than that. In fact, I refuse to trade in a car until I have driven it to Tranquility Base. The geek in me still rules.

By comparison, Mars is between 54.6 million and 401 million kilometers from the earth, because Mars very inconveniently orbits the sun, not us. And you can't travel straight from here to there for the same reason. It is a more challenging trip by many orders of magnitude.

Lifting a payload into earth's orbit requires reaching escape velocity, which is 40,270 kilometers/hour. That's really fast. And it really consumes a lot of fuel. Then, you've got to take that payload a few hundred million kilometers to the Red Planet, land it safely somehow, and have enough fuel and supplies for the return trip, along with a few Martian rocks. Adding people, food, oxygen, and a few amenities for a trip that long adds a lot of weight. You get the picture.

Business magnate/visionary Elon Musk thinks he can send tourists on a round-trip to Mars for a paltry $200,000 each. I cannot fathom how he can pull that off and shudder to think what would be on the menu for those making that months-long journey. But there are a lot of things I do not understand, like how someone could start a company making battery-powered cars that has done nothing but lose money, and still be worth billions.

Then there's the radiation. There's no practical way to build a spaceship that can shield passengers from it, and people making the journey to Mars would almost surely receive a dose, coming and going, that would keep an oncologist busy upon their return to Earth.

Then, you've got to deal with the bad press if there's a technical failure, which will surely be fatal if it happens. That would bring a fate even worse than death: congressional hearings.

So the solution is obvious: cut the cost, and risk, of the trip roughly in half by making it one-way only.

I can't take credit for this idea. Mars One, a not for profit outfit in the Netherlands, is already taking applications. I would sign up in a heartbeat if my deafness and lack of any useful skills would not disqualify me outright.

Neil Armstrong was 38 years old when he stepped onto the lunar surface. He had more than half of his life ahead of him, as it turned out (he died in 2012). It would have been a tragedy had he died on the return trip.

Not so tragic if you send someone old, like me. I'm a depreciated asset, like a car that's been driven 384,400 kilometers. Some days ahead, yes, but the bulk of life is in the rear-view mirror.

So, send your best and brightest to Mars, as long as they qualify for AARP membership. Make it a one-way trip and give them a teary goodbye at the launch pad.

The Mars mission would have one overriding objective, of course: to transport extremophiles to the Martian surface and seed it with life. Bugs and tiny photosynthesizers that live in Earth's polar regions would probably do well on Mars, particularly if they could be engineered to be tolerant of radiation (Mars, unfortunately, lacks a strong magnetic field). There would be no greater human accomplishment, in my estimation, than to be the fly that walks across that petri dish. I would happily nourish the living goo with my own remains at the conclusion of my days on Mars.

Once the genie of life has gotten out of the bottle, it will take on a life of its own, so to speak. Over enough millennia, Mars would almost certainly become more earth-like by its presence. Perhaps Mars will be habitable by humans someday. Or maybe real Martians will evolve from the seeds we plant there and colonize Earth eons from now, after we humans have driven ourselves to extinction fighting pointless religious wars.

Stephen Hawking and quite a number of other great minds believe that we need to colonize Mars for the survival of our species. We're so stubbornly self-destructive, the reasoning goes, that we'll double our chances of survival by moving to Mars. Besides, the sun is heating up.

This reasoning is wrong-headed. There are much cheaper ways to save our species from a catastrophic war, plague from an antibiotic-resistant superbug, or meteor strike. We could create a "doomsday seed bank" for humans, staffed by a skeletal crew of real humans who would unite sperm and eggs as soon as Armageddon sets in and raise a new generation of people to repeat the process of self-destruction. But I could be wrong. As the "Goldilocks Zone" shifts further out from the sun, maybe the descendants of Elon Musk will find a billion-year stay of execution on Mars, where a brighter sun and more efficient solar panels might finally make the Tesla a practical ride.

Regardless of its value to the future of humanity, Mars would become a lot more interesting place with life on it. Here on earth, invasive species find new homes all the time by being transported in the bilge water of human tankers, in the bellies of human aircraft, or on the soles of human feet. It wouldn't take much effort for humans to give life a beachhead on the Red Planet.

I think I could manage to spend my golden years living in a lava tube 15 degrees north of the Martian equator. It would remind me of a giant wine cellar. A Martian day is 24 hours and 37 minutes long, and I'm confident that I could adjust to sleeping a few extra minutes every day. And I would weigh a lot less—about 62% less—without shedding mass. My joints would not ache as much as they do here on Earth.

Among the best things about living on Mars would be the fact that I could recalculate my age. A Martian year is 687 days. By that measure, I am barely past my 30th birthday. I could spend the rest of my days hanging out with 30-somethings and not feel old.

Finally, I would never have to ever fill out another Form 1040, with all of its odious schedules which have aged me so considerably here on Earth. But thanks to tax cheat Charles Rangel, as an American citizen I would be still subject to US taxation on Mars and potentially prevented from opening up a bank account there. Such is the US Tax Code. I can't make this up.

But as an extraterrestrial ex-pat, I would be comfortably beyond the practical reach of even the IRS. Yes, thanks to Charles Rangel, the IRS could audit me from Earth, perhaps busting me for filing a Form 1040 (electronically, obviously) that fails to declare imputed income for living rent-free in a lava tube. But at least they wouldn't be able to garnish my oxygen.

It would be a journey worth taking. I would be a free man at last.

Afterword: The Days of Future Passed

I've come to the end of this particular journey, and story. You can put a book down after reading it and pick it up to enjoy it another day. People are not as lucky as books. People only get one chance to live and die.

Although life's experiences may be recorded while alive, it is impossible to authoritatively write about the experience of death. Since death is inevitable, this leaves us much to contemplate. Is death really the end?

As an atheist, I accept the end as the end, and I do so with equanimity. The alternative is to hitch your wagon to a deity whose existence can neither be proved nor disproved and swallow an improbable accompanying dogma that prescribes a hedonistic image of an afterlife. For jihadists, it is the image of an eternity spent in the company of 40 virgins. For Catholics, it is the "beatific vision" that serves as our reward for spending a lifetime eschewing meat on Fridays. For an atheist like me, what comes to mind is the final absurd dining room scene from the Monty Python film, "The Meaning of Life."

So why should I, or any atheist, care about experiencing the inevitable? Or, for that matter, care about the future of what we leave behind?

If we atheists were as self-absorbed as Donald Trump, we would live life large to our very last day, and blow whatever's left on a big funeral and an ostentatious, gilded gravestone that would be mounted on a beautiful promontory with a view of water. We would do that just to rob that view from others, out of spite. Graveyards set in beautiful places are a waste of good, developable land. Dead people can't appreciate the view.

Mercifully, most people are not so self-absorbed, even the ones who don't believe in an afterlife. Non-believers do, in fact, care about what they leave behind, as illogical as that may seem to believers. That's "secular humanism" in a nutshell. Maybe it's because we know this is our only chance to make things right.

For me, I imagine the death experience to be much like falling into a black hole. From the outside, the moment of death would be easily recorded as one slips beyond the event horizon. But from the inside, it would seem timeless.

These days, I frequently find myself pondering what the world will be like without me. I think, with some degree of regret, that the place would not notice my absence at all and would be no better off as a result of the days that I spent here.

It follows, then, that I have already begun the process of dying.

I see unmistakable evidence of that, because the world is moving a lot faster now than it used to be. My driving hasn't changed, but compared to others on the road, I've slowed down. I can still communicate effectively with the people around me, but I have trouble keeping up with the topics of conversation that amuse young people these days, and I tax the patience of those who must endure my musings and tired stories. That's why I spend a lot of my free time in the company of old men like Dino and away from the shrill voices of females.

Thus, becoming a curmudgeon is just an early stage of death. It's a change in perspective that is the consequence of falling into that black hole, one that shifts attention from the short-term to something longer.

Compared to my youth, little troubles me these days. My kids are all educated and emancipated, and two have begun producing children of their own. I can remember all of their birthdays, which is good, but they seem to come a lot faster than they used to. There're more of them to remember, as my genes become simultaneously preserved and diluted.

Seasons pass more quickly, too. The three months between the autumnal equinox and the winter solstice brings a profound change of weather in Kentuckiana, which now seems to happen overnight. The first chill of autumn sends me reaching for some warmer garments, which are easy to find because I never got around to packing them away the previous spring.

From the perspective of someone falling into a black hole, life may be likened to roll of paper towels. Every sheet wipes up after a day of gustatory indulgences, which pass at a constant speed. But the roll spins faster toward the end. Ultimately, everything disappears down the hole.

Falling into a black hole requires that you set goals that are reasonable and achievable. Write a book, put the town of Story onto the National Register of Historic Places, witness the birth of a grandchild, visit a new winery or an old friend. Things like that.

So what's to become of the world after we cross the event horizon?

Life on the outside will go on, quite literally. Life has had a tenacious grip on this planet for about 3.6 billion years, and it will be here, regulating the earth's climate, atmosphere and seas until the sun becomes a bloated red giant about 4 billion years from now. That's James Lovelock's Gaia Hypothesis in a nutshell, and to a person who sees things around him speeding up, I now see validation of it everywhere.

Humans are not so tenacious. If past is prologue, species survive, on average, about one million years. Successful ones like ours have a shorter tenure on average. That's because successful species tend to alter the very conditions needed for their continued survival. We humans are certainly doing that. But at least we're waking up to that reality, so we might yet beat the odds.

By far, the biggest threat to human survival is humans. As Pogo said, "We have met the enemy, and he is us." Will we be smart enough not to succumb to tribal conflict and senseless religious wars? I'm not so sure.

Humans will continue to evolve. They never stopped evolving.

We Americans are aborting a lot of future criminals as well as Downs babies these days. Countries like China are tampering with human reproduction in novel ways, and we will see the long-term effects of that. The Flynn Effect may make us smarter, eventually, but human evolution is already in hyper drive anyway as we incorporate technology into our personal lives. Our symbiosis with machines will have profound and unpredictable consequences.

When I was a kid, a telephone was a clunky device with a rotary dial, tethered to a wall. Today, everyone carries around a supercomputer that wirelessly performs the same function and many others. We have already evolved into creatures that are not purely biological in nature.

Those supercomputers enable the NSA to monitor everywhere we go, and everything we communicate, data which is preserved for posterity in a super-sized supercomputer located near Bluffdale, Utah. The future predicted by George Orwell has already come to pass, without our even noticing.

Artificial intelligence may pose a threat, as computing power continues to grow as predicted by Moore's Law. Stephen Hawking thinks so. By their nature, computers are very patient and tolerant, so they may be willing to share the planet with us. Perhaps smart computers will protect us against our own folly, and refuse to obey our commands to them to slaughter our own kind.

The weather will change. So will climate. Glaciations occur about every 100,000 years, and Kentuckiana will once again sit at the edge of, or under, another massive glacier.

Human bones will, finally, find their way into sedimentary rock, along with polyethylene microbeads from Crest toothpaste.

Continents will continue to drift. North America is gradually moving westward. In a few million years, the sun will rise an hour later in Kentuckiana. A day will be a few minutes longer, too.

But some things will never change.

> The United States will always have but two viable political parties, neither one of which will offer good governance.
>
> AT&T will always be a rent-seeking oligopoly.
>
> We will never be able to order just the cable/satellite channels we want to watch.
>
> Despite the "Flynn Effect," no human will ever be able to fully understand the United States Tax Code.
>
> People will continue to believe in absurdities, and that will cause them to commit atrocities.
>
> Indiana will never allow the carry-out sale of beer on Sundays.

And the people of Kentuckiana will always eat corn.

Kentickiana Picture Credits

1. Baptism at Pike's Peak, circa 1916, Frank Hohenberger, Brown County Historical Society
2. Delivery Wagon with hard tires at Story's General Store, circa 1920, photographer unknown, picture found at the Story Inn.
3. Map of Kentuckiana illustrated by Dani Ham, 2017.
4. Unpaved road to Story, Frank Hohenberger, Brown County Historical Society
5. Game Wardens Oliver Neal and son Fred Neal with captured still at "Weed Patch Hill" (now in Brown County State Park), July 22, 1926, Frank Hohenberger, Brown County Historical Society
6. Two Story farmhouse at Story, circa 1920, Frank Hohenberger, Lilly Library, Indiana University Bloomington, IN
7. Old Clapboard Schoolhouse at Story, circa 1920, Frank Hohenberger, Lilly Library, Indiana University, Bloomington, IN
8. Bean Blossom Covered Bridge, date unknown, Frank Hohenberger, Brown County Historical Society
9. Gnaw Bone road sign, date unknown, photographer unknown, Brown County Historical Society
10. "Van Buren Wave", illustrated by Dani Ham, 2017
11. Marguerite Rust at Stone Head, circa 1914, Frank Hohenberger, Brown County Historical Society
12. Baptism at New Bellesville near Lon Clark Bridge, March 1915, Frank Hohenberger, Brown County Historical Society
13. Doctor Ralphy's examination room, date unknown, Frank Hohenberger, Brown County Historical Society
14. Horse-drawn hearse, date unknown, Frank Hohenberger, Lilly

Library, Indiana University, Bloomington, IN

15. Jane Story's gravestone at Christianburg Cemetery, picture taken by Jane Simon Ammeson, 2016

16. Forrest Lucas, date unknown, family picture provided by his sister Carol Cummins

17. Liar's Bench in downtown Nashville, circa 1933, Frank Hohenberger, Brown County Historical Society

18. Brown County Sheriff, date unknown, Frank Hohenberger, Brown County Historical Society

19. Story's General Store, circa 1910, Frank Hohenberger, Lilly Library, Indiana University, Bloomington, IN

20. Alra Wheeler in front of the "new" General Store at Story, circa 1916, photographer unknown, picture found at the Story Inn

21. Brown County Sheriff Clarence "Nub" Moore (left) and deputies with still captured at Story, pictured in front of the Nashville jail, November 16, 1928, Frank Hohenberger, Lilly Library, Indiana University, Bloomington, IN

22. Deckard School pupils drinking from creek, date unknown, Frank Hohenberger, Lilly Library, Indiana University, Bloomington, IN

23. Dick Jones with rifle in downtown Nashville, circa 1930's, Frank Hohenberger, Lilly Library, Indiana University, Bloomington, IN

24. Dr. Ralphy and his pupils at the Story School, date unknown, photographer unknown, picture found at the Story Inn

25. Panning for gold in Spearsville, July 24, 1929, Frank Hohenberger, Lilly Library, Indiana University, Bloomington, IN

26. Sheriff Clint Moore (right) and deputies with captured still at Nashville's Old Log Jail, circa 1920, Frank Hohenberger, Lilly Library, Indiana University, Bloomington, IN

27. Brown County Homesteaders, date unknown, Frank Hohenberger, Brown County Historical Society

28. Mary Ford and Herbert McDonald with huckster wagon stuck in mud, July 13, 1937, Frank Hohenberger, Lilly Library, Indiana University, Bloomington, IN

29. Pig farmer Bert Laurie, 1930's, photographer unknown, Brown County Historical Society

30. Gravestone of Sister Angela Benedict taken at Oldenburg cemetery, Rick Hofstetter, 2016

31. Alra Wheeler and family at Story, circa 1905, photographer unknown, picture found at Story Inn

Printed in the United States
By Bookmasters